THE HISTORY OF COSTA RICA

THE
HISTORY
OF

COSTA RICA

BRIEF, UP-TO-DATE AND ILLUSTRATED

SECOND EDITION REVISED

Iván Molina
Steven Palmer

EDITORIAL
UCR
2014

972.86
M722h2   Molina Jiménez, Iván, 1961-
              The history of Costa Rica : brief, up-to-date and illustra-
          ted / Iván Molina, Steven Palmer. – 2. ed., 4ª. reimpr. – San
          José, C.R. : Edit. UCR, 2014.
              x, 218 p. : il., mapas.

          ISBN 978-9968-46-023-1

              1. COSTA RICA – HISTORIA. I. Palmer, Steven Paul,
          1961-   , coautor II. Título.

          CIP/2603
          CC/SIBDI.UCR

Edition approved by the Comisión Editorial de la Universidad de Costa Rica

Second edition: 2007
Fourth reprinted: 2014

Cover desing: Boris Valverde G.
Layout: *Iván Molina.*

© Editorial Universidad de Costa Rica, Ciudad Universitaria Rodrigo Facio. Costa Rica.
P.O. Box 11501-2060 • Tel.: 2511 5310 · Fax: 2511 5257 • administracion.siedin@ucr.ac.cr • www.editorial.ucr.ac.cr

CONTENTS

Prologue
An Excursion to the Past   ix

Chapter 1
Trails of the First Peoples
(12,000 B.C.-1500 A.D.)   1

Chapter 2
Cacicazgos and *Señorios*
(1500-1570)   11

Chapter 3
Conquest and Resistance
(1502-1570)   19

Chapter 4
The Early Colonial World
(1570-1700)   29

Chapter 5
Merchants and Peasants
(1700-1850)   39

Chapter 6
Coffee, Capitalism and the
Liberal State (1850-1890)   63

Chapter 7
Diversification, Conflict and
Democracy (1890-1930)   77

Chapter 8
The Depression, Social Reform
and Civil War (1930-1950)   99

Chapter 9
The Golden Age of the Middle
Class (1950-1978)   119

Chapter 10
Recent Past, Near
Future   145

Epilogue
Costa Rican
Exceptionalism   181

Chronology   183

Bibliography   193

Illustrations   201

Index   207

Authors   217

AN EXCURSION TO
THE PAST

This brief history, the first of its kind in the English language, offers readers from all parts of the world a condensed and illustrated account of Costa Rica's past. Its pages focus on the principal events and patterns in the country's colorful and exceptional history. The story begins in ancient times when the tropical forests hid the elusive footsteps of primitive hunters, and brings us to the ever more urban and complex present. The sweep is wide, ranging from the domestication of plants between 4,000 and 1,000 B.C., to the Civil War of 1948, and from the rise of the coffee and banana industries in the nineteenth century to the tourism boom of the 1990s.

Travelers.

The book is not a publicity pamphlet promoting Costa Rica's natural

In January [1915], *the time had come to leave San José and go to Nicaragua... As I look back, however, I think that my stay in Costa Rica was in some ways the pleasantest part of my Central American experience, though not the most interesting. There was no other country where I felt that I was participating so fully in the social life of the community, and none where I found people more attractive and more friendly.*

Dana Gardner Munro, US scholar and diplomat, 1983.

wonders to tourists. Instead, this slim volume invites the reader to get to know the essential background and characteristics of a country that undermines stereotypes about Latin America. In some ways the invitation is similar to those extended every day by travel agencies and tour companies, but in this case the excursion is not to a volcano, to a beach, or to an island – this tour is a journey into the past.

Sign on and you will head out on safari with primitive hunters, observe the everyday labors of the tribal societies of the sixteenth century, and participate in the Conquest. You will sojourn through colonial villages, experience the expansion of coffee farming after 1830, and witness the boom of banana cultivation in the virgin jungles of the late nineteenth century. And, as the tour brings us back to our point of departure, you will watch a nation take shape and a democracy take root, participate in the protests of peasants, artisans and workers, and get a close-up look at the crisis of 1930 and the conflict of 1948. Finally, you will visit the ruins of Costa Rica's social democratic dream (1950-78), and enjoy an afternoon of shopping in the malls of a neoliberal and thoroughly postmodern tropical republic at the dawn of the 21st century.

Fasten your seat-belt – some turbulence is expected – and have a pleasant trip.

CHAPTER 1

TRAILS OF THE FIRST PEOPLES (12,000 B.C.-1500 A.D.)

Bands of primitive people who specialized in hunting began to occupy America about forty thousand years ago. The immigrants came from Asia, crossing the Bering Straits and occupying the north-western part of the continent. Gradually, over a period of thousands of years, they moved southwards. The everyday life of these small, nomadic bands of close kin was taken up by hunting, gathering and fishing in rivers, lakes and oceans. They knew nothing about growing foodstuffs, and their division of labor scarcely went beyond criteria of age and sex.

The territory that is now Costa Rica was likely occupied between 12,000 and 8,000 B.C. The early settlers inhabited a landscape dominated

Arrowheads, Turrialba,
12,000-8,000 B.C.

Scraping instruments, Turrialba, 12,000-8,000 B.C.

by tropical forests. Some of the animals they hunted became extinct a long time ago: mastodons, giant sloths, horses and camelids. Their tools were made from stone (especially silica), wood, hides and bones. By and large, these objects were designed for hunting: a variety of pointed projectiles, hammers, scrapers, knives and chisels, for example.

Between 8,000 and 4,000 B.C., these early inhabitants tended to become sedentary. Either by accident, or by picking up knowledge from neighboring groups, they learned to domesticate plants. Archaeologists have found evidence that settlements were increasingly made up of more people and had greater permanence. At the same time, in the course of repeated gathering in the same forests, these primitive peoples acquired experience that allowed a gradual selection of certain varieties of plants and animals for human consumption.

The transition to farming was a slow process that extended between 4,000 and 1,000 years before Christ. Costa Rica's position on the isthmus made it a meeting place of North and South American cultural currents. This allowed the inhabitants to acquire knowledge about the domestication of root vegetables like yucca and sweet potato common in the tropical areas of South America, as well as to learn about the growing of grains like corn, more typical of the semi-arid zones of Mexico. The influence was itself geographically marked: on the Caribbean side, where contact with South America was common, the cultivation of tubers predominated; corn and beans were prevalent in the Central Valley and in the Pacific north, areas that related more with the northern cultures.

Hunting turtles.

With the domestication of agriculture came changes in the instruments of labor. Grinding and nutcracking stones, as well as other tools for processing vegetables, were supplemented by objects for better exploiting the forests, such as axes, hatchets and levers. The use of a variety of organic products (wood, teeth, shells and bamboo) also intensified, at the same time that pottery for preparing and storing food became more sophisticated. The typical product of the potter's hands was the *tecomate*, a large vessel with a narrow mouth used for storing foodstuffs.

Between 1,000 B.C. and 800 A.D., the early societies underwent decisive changes. The principal one was the consolidation of agriculture, which gathered momentum at the expense of the most basic survival activities (hunting, fishing and gathering). Notable at first was the planting of root vegetables, yucca being the most common, which was associated with the creation of more specialized artifacts such as *budares*, large ceramic dishes used to cook the root. The cultivation of corn, at first simply one among many agricultural activities, successfully expanded in the five hundred years before Christ.

At the same time that they permitted population growth, advances in the production of foodstuffs reinforced sedentary habits. This in turn was the basis of growing knowledge that came from the daily observation of flora and fauna as they were being domesticated. Permanence stimulated the diversification of crafts, and artisans began to dedicate themselves to fashioning objects beyond those necessary for survival: necklaces, *metates* (smooth stones for grinding with elaborately sculpted bases), multi-colored ceramics and *ocarinas*. Sedentary living also demanded that a greater amount of territory be accessible so that cultivation might be rotated as soils were depleted.

Figure on a *metate* (used for preparing food), Pacific north, 500-800 A.D.

Social and political organization changed alongside the transformation of production methods. The basic change was the passage from the small band, dedicated to hunting, fishing and gathering, to the tribe. The tribe had a greater populace, it specialized in agriculture and it inhabited a defined territory. Essentially, as a village subdivided on the basis of population growth, it gave origin to other village units, with which it would generally unite in a confederation. Kinship networks were the axis of this complex and intermittent process.

The egalitarian character of the first villages disappeared as the division of labor increased and a hierarchy of villages took shape. Aside from spurring population growth, the production of an agricultural surplus promoted the rise of specialized roles, such as administrators for organizing the distribution of the bounty of the land, and warriors for defending the territory. Equally important were functions linked to the cult of the ancestors and other religious activities. During the first 500 years after Christ, a social hierarchy emerged, with the figure of the *cacique* (or chief) at the top. Power and wealth became concentrated in certain settlements.

The links between villages of different size and status, which together marked off a specific territory, were the basis of the *cacicazgos* (chieftainships).

Figure of a shaman, Atlantic area, 500-1000 A.D.

These early political associations were also the basis of commerce, which involved some surprisingly long-distance trade. The settlers of the Caribbean and Pacific south regions of the country were part of the mercantile circuits of their neighbors in Panama, Colombia and Ecuador.

Indigenous vessel.

In Nicoya, the northern influence of Mesoamerican (Mexican and Central American) indigenous groups was more prominent. The groups of Costa Rica's Central Valley benefited from the influence of both poles. The merchandise coming from Costa Rican territory was not of great importance to this extensive network of exchange; it was essentially confined to perishable articles like salt, cocoa beans, quetzal feathers and dyes made from crushed shells. Mesoamerican traditions lost strength between 500 and 800 A.D.

Southern cultures took advantage of this to broaden their influence throughout Costa Rican territory. The change was most clearly registered in craftwork. Jade sculpting, which had followed Mayan models, was displaced by the working of metals, especially gold. The lovely gold jewelry and adornments for warrior garb had shapes and styles similar to those found in Panama and Colombia. The available evidence, although fragmentary, confirms that the first peoples of Costa Rica were very influenced by the Chibcha civilization.

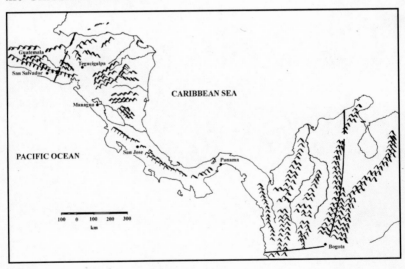

Area of Chibcha influence, c. 800 A.D.

Costa Rican southern communities created sculptures whose meaning and function remain an enigma to archaeologists, leading to comparisons with the monoliths of Stonehenge and the gargantuan heads of Easter Island: huge stone spheres, of an almost perfect roundness, some exceed a meter and a half in height and weigh tons. Specialists think that they were used to mark status and territorial limits, and also postulate an association with religion, astronomy, and the agricultural cycle.

Stone sphere in the National Museum, Pacific south, 1-500 A.D.

The system of *cacicazgos* flourished in the 750 years prior to Conquest by the Spaniards (from about 800 to 1550 A.D.). The system's splendor came from a more intensive production of grains and roots, which combined the use of natural fertilizers and irrigation with the slashing and burning of the forests to prepare fields for agriculture. Farming was complemented by hunting and fishing, and by the gathering of salt, fruits, beeswax and honey. As the principal settlements grew, acquiring aqueducts, roads, bridges, houses, temples and palisades for defence, they need a more diverse set of artisanal skills.

Indigenous community.

As *cacicazgos* became larger, social differentiation increased. Inevitably, a military and religious nobility was consolidated. The nobles ruled over workers and slaves, these latter usually prisoners captured in tribal conflicts. Kinship networks and the principle of reciprocity (fair exchange of goods among equals) were outweighed by this political hierarchy, which allowed shamans and warriors to exploit their social inferiors. Charged with regulating everyday life, these elites arranged the distribution of riches, power and knowledge in their favor. This model of domination was well established by the sixteenth century when indigenous societies had to face rivals far different from any enemy they had known to that point.

Warrior with axe and head, Atlantic area, 500-1000 A.D.

CHAPTER 2

CACICAZGOS AND *SEÑORÍOS* (1500-1570)

On the eve of the Spanish Conquest of Costa Rica, diverse indigenous societies were dispersed throughout south-eastern Central America. They were politically fragmented, and neither their social organization nor their use of technology was sophisticated in comparison with the better known Mayan indigenous groups of northern Central America.

The civilizations of the Guatemalan and Salvadoran highlands, and of the lowlands of the Yucatan Peninsula and the Gulf of Honduras, had large and dense populations, and displayed great cultural diversity. For the most part Mayan, by the sixteenth century these peoples had become strongly influenced by Mexican cultures. The ruins of the Mayan cities are spectacular records of

Indigenous people in the forest.

the urban growth, the architectural techniques, the precise knowledge of astronomy and the artistic vision that graced this civilization. Mayan, and later Aztec, influence was felt far to the south, and shaped some elements of Costa Rica's pre-Columbian cultures.

At the beginning of the sixteenth century some hundreds of thousands indigenous people lived in the territory that would become Costa Rica. The majority of them were located in the Pacific north-west and in the Central Valley. The population growth that had come with more intensive agriculture (that of corn in particular) did not lead to any drastic transformation of the landscape. The aboriginal peoples made room for themselves in a lush tropical wilderness, characterized by impenetrable forests, vigorous rivers, daunting swamps, exuberant vegetation, dense mountain ranges and animal life that was diverse and often savage.

The village was the basis of indigenous civilization. It was the axis of everyday life, which was taken up by agriculture, crafts, commerce and war. Once conjoined in a federation, the villages became local cells of a *cacicazgo*, or chieftainship. The place each *cacicazgo* occupied in the hierarchy of regional political power varied according to the size of its population and of the territory under its control. Beyond this, a *cacicazgo* could integrate itself

The roughest mountains I have ever seen and, in the opinion of some, the roughest that have ever been seen. Intolerable conditions of hunger and thirst slowed our attempts to slice open narrow pathways, and to climb and descend great peaks, so cavernous and drenched in rain that the sight of the sun was a marvel.

Juan Vázquez de Coronado, one of the conquistadors of Costa Rica, 1563.

into a larger, more centralized political and military unit called a *señorío*, a kind of fiefdom with jurisdiction over a vast and disputed territory.

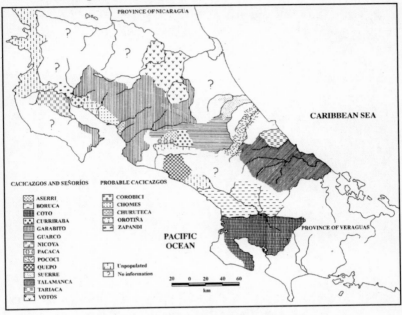

Cacicazgos and *señoríos* of Costa Rica, 16th century.

On the eve of Conquest, the *cacicazgo* of Nicoya was the most important in Costa Rica's Pacific north. Other principal chieftainships were the Votos of the San Carlos plains, near the present border with Nicaragua; the Suerre, Pococí, Tariaca and Talamanca of the Caribbean lowlands; the Quepo, Coto and Boruca of the Pacific south; and the *señoríos* of Guarco and Garabito in the Central Valley. Guarco territory was concentrated to the east of present-day Cartago, though it also included areas between Alajuela and San José. The domains of the Garabito extended from Esparza to the banks of the San Juan River.

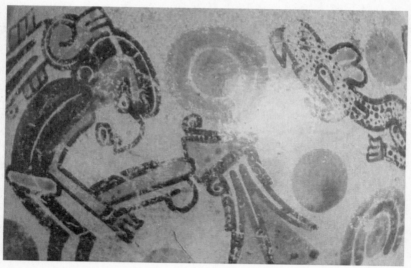

Sacred struggle between light and darkness (detail), Pacific north, 800-1350 A.D.

An indigenous nobility ruled over these different types of territorial organizations. At the top of the largest political entities were lords, while lesser federations were ruled by principal and secondary *caciques*. The nobility was united by kinship ties, and its authority was enhanced by claims to special religious and magical powers. These noble leaders fulfilled particular roles with regard to warfare, commerce and relations with supernatural beings. In doing so, they consolidated privileged positions that allowed them to exploit their social inferiors, and to gain access to gold and slaves. Political power was inherited through matrilineal succession, and the origins of that power were associated with venerable ancestors, a mythical weight that increased the respect for noble lineage.

Indigenous Dwelling in Sipurio, Talamanca. Oil on canvas. Luis Sanclemente, 1892.

There were notable cultural differences among the many indigenous groups of Costa Rica. Architecturally, the elliptical house prevailed in the Pacific north, while a circular dwelling was common in the Central Valley. In marked contrast to these, the typical construction of the Caribbean side and in the Pacific south was the *palenque*, a kind of longhouse protected by stockades and capable of housing 300 to 400 people. The linguistic terrain was also varied. Since oral communication predominated, the small region had a large number of languages. It is likely, however, that Huetar, the language used by the *señoríos* of Garabito and Guarco, had become a lingua franca for many other tribes.

The religion of the indigenous groups was animist. They believed that people, animals and natural phenomena all had spirits, and that these spirits could be bad, damaging or dangerous. Funeral rites displayed expectations of immortality. Special treatment was given to the corpse, particularly when it belonged to a member of the nobility. The dead were buried with different objects (sometimes even gold objects), and with their slaves who were sacrificed for the occasion so that they might continue serving their master or mistress in the next life.

Religious activities took place in temples, similar to the dwellings but larger in size. These sacred places also served to house ritual objects: musical instruments, masks and mats. They were the site of ceremonies where priests professed the cults of certain icons (which were made of gold, to judge by the way the Spanish sacked these temples). The shaman fulfilled various crucial functions: he answered the queries of the community, foretold the future, and served as intermediary between the supernatural realm and that of everyday life.

In the sixteenth century, human sacrifice and cannibalism were practiced in

The Tuarco chief [was with]... an Indian wrapped in blankets, with gold and other things, above a barbecue... More than sixty Indian men and many Indian women were wailing according to their funeral custom. It made me sad to think that four days earlier they had killed four or six boys in order to bury them along with the dead chief.

Juan Vázquez de Coronado, 1563.

Costa Rica's Pacific north. The *caci-cazgo* of Nicoya organized such ritual celebrations three times a year, coinciding with the corn harvests. On the day of the festival, with the nobility dressed in full regalia and painted for the occasion, a ceremonial mixture of alcohol – *chicha* – was drunk, and expressive dances were performed before the temple. Then five or six people of either sex, previously selected, were brought to the altar at the top of the temple, their hearts cut out, their heads chopped off, and their bodies rolled down the side of the temple so that their flesh could be consumed with all the solemnity of the moment.

Human sacrifice during funeral rites or harvest ceremonies was directly related to the military sphere, since warfare was the principal source of the slaves. War was constant and widespread. Sometimes groups went to war to defend or to expand their territory. They might also fight to gain or maintain access to important trade routes, or to acquire gold through pillage. Other times, wars were fought to impose – or to oppose – patterns of unequal exchange, or they resulted from a scarcity of food or materials that might occur after natural disasters or political conflicts. War was also undertaken to steal adults and children. Prisoners added to the labor force, and women of fertile age gave their captors'

They take a woman or man... and lead him up the mount and open up his side and extract his heart, and the first blood is sacrificed to the sun. Then they decapitate the man along with four or five others on a stone... and they throw the corpses over the side to roll down, where they are collected and subsequently eaten as sacred and valued food.

Gonzalo Fernández de Oviedo, 1527.

tribes greater potential for population growth.

War also had a variety of magical dimensions. Robbing the gold of a rival band weakened them, for example, and enemies were decapitated and their severed heads used as trophies. The arms employed in warfare were bows, arrows, spears, stones and shields made of wood or of hides. Among the battle tactics were ambushes, the use of traps, surprise attacks, plunder, and the burning of crops and villages. Military success depended on the alliances that could be forged between the contenders and their neighbors. This was a traditional strategy that was extremely useful for the Spanish during the Conquest.

The end of one civilization and the beginning of another.

CHAPTER 3

CONQUEST AND RESISTANCE (1502-1570)

The Spanish subjugation of Costa Rica came late in the conquest of Central America, and it was never really completed. The conquistadors were actually preceded by the arrival of their viruses and bacteria, which began to decimate the indigenous populations. Though the Costa Rican education system has propagated the myth that there were virtually no indigenous people in the territory when the Spanish arrived, in fact there were approximately 400,000 – a figure that would not be matched by the Hispanic, mestizo populace of Costa Rica until the 1920s. By 1569, once the Spaniards had managed to gain a permanent foothold, there were only 120,000 indigenous people, and by 1611 there were a mere 10,000 left.

Indigenous resistance.

The most damage to the native people was wrought by epidemic diseases caused by contact with invaders from another continent. The immune systems of the indigenous groups were incapable of dealing with new viruses like smallpox, typhus, whooping cough, measles and influenza. This human catastrophe was exacerbated by warfare and the horrific exploitation of indigenous labor.

Much of Central America was conquered between 1519 and 1525. There were two converging waves: one moving south from Mexico and another heading north from Panama. The fact that Central America's indigenous groups were so politically fragmented made Spanish control extremely difficult. Spanish efforts to consolidate their power were further complicated by endless conflicts among the invaders themselves. This political chaos was the backdrop to the region's first economic "boom" between 1536 and 1540 which was based on the genocidal enslavement of the indigenous groups of Nicoya and Nicaragua, exported in huge numbers to the Antilles, the Gulf of Honduras, Peru and Panama.

The political organization of Central America was stabilized between 1540 and 1570. In 1548, the *Audiencia* of Santiago de Guatemala was founded, and from 1570 onwards it had jurisdiction over all the territory

In one single ship that was carrying [to Peru?] four hundred Indian men and women [slaves], not fifty were left by the end of the voyage, for the rest had all expired.

Act prohibiting the export of indigenous people from Nicaragua and Nicoya, 1536.

stretching between Chiapas (currently on the Mexican side of the border with Guatemala) and Bocas del Toro (present-day Panama). Costa Rica was divided into two jurisdictions, the Province of Costa Rica and the Corregimiento of Nicoya. The Kingdom of Guatemala, as it was also known, was an administrative entity that had a great deal of autonomy from the powerful Viceroyalty of New Spain (Mexico), and the region was able to preserve that separate status throughout the colonial period.

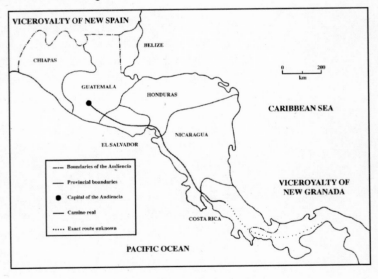

Audiencia of Guatemala, c. 1800.

Civil and ecclesiastical officials exercised the greatest authority within this new institutional framework. They were most in control in the highlands, and on the piedmont and coastal plains of the Pacific side of the isthmus. The Caribbean side remained virtually unconquered, given its distance from the main population centers, its uncomfortable climate and the tenacious resistance of its indigenous groups.

The initial phase of Costa Rica's conquest was part of the Spanish effort to subdue the Pacific side of Central America. In 1519, Hernán Ponce de León reached the Gulf of Nicoya, but he did not disembark; in 1522, Gil González Dávila explored the area by land and traded with the indigenous groups; and in 1524, Francisco Fernández de Córdoba founded Villa Bruselas. This first settlement of the Spanish invaders on Costa Rican soil was short-lived. It disappeared in 1527, due to disputes among the conquistadors and aboriginal attacks which forced the last settlers to abandon the site.

Exploration of Costa Rican Pacific coast.

Although the town had a brief life, its foundation inaugurated a violent dismantling of the *cacicazgos* of the Pacific north-west. Apart from being exported as slaves, indigenous people were distributed among the conquerors in *encomiendas*, a kind of serfdom that obliged native people to provide labor and goods to their *encomendero*. The local indigenous nobility often collaborated with the conquistadors. This limited the possibilities for concerted armed resistance by

Costa Rica's first peoples, who sometimes opted for flight into the mountainous forests. Figures from Nicoya that show a drop in the number of men of working age from 2,000 in 1529 to 500 in 1557 offer more evidence of the devastating effect of the Spanish invasion.

On the Caribbean side of the territory, the conquest was even more violent – and even less successful. Columbus landed in present-day Limón in 1502, but the first, disastrous exploration of the coast was carried out in 1510 by Diego de Nicuesa. His early example was imitated twenty years later by Felipe Gutiérrez (1534-35), and subsequently by Hernán Sánchez de Badajoz (1539-41), Rodrigo de Contreras (1540-41) and Diego Gutiérrez (1543-44). The aboriginals, friendly at first, began to offer military resistance to the invaders once the Spanish started to demand food and gold.

In their desire to subdue the people on the Caribbean coast, the conquistadors founded Villa de la Concepción in 1535, and Badajoz and Marbella in 1540, amongst other settlements. All were ephemeral. These efforts failed due to conflicts among the Spaniards, difficult terrain, an incapacity to endure the climate, the complexity of receiving supplies from other parts of the isthmus and fierce indigenous resistance. This violent resistance

I arrived in the land of Cariay [in 1502], where I stopped to mend and provision the ships, and to give some rest to the crew members who were quite ill... There I heard tales of the gold mines that I was searching for in the province of Ciamba.

Christopher Columbus, letter written in Jamaica, July 1503.

was a result of the Spaniards' tendency to mistreat rather than to co-opt the hierarchy of chiefs. More dispersed and fragmented than their counterparts in the Pacific north, the native people also enjoyed the cover of the thick forests, and they did not hesitate to pull up their crops in order to make the invading forces withdraw for lack of food.

Whipping and dismemberment of indigenous people.

The death of Diego Gutiérrez at the hands of indigenous people (1544) was the beginning of a long hiatus in the process of conquest in this part of the country. The next attempt to conquer the Caribbean side began in 1560, when the cleric Juan de Estrada Rávago left Granada, Nicaragua, and reached Bocas del Toro, where he founded the town of Castillo de Austria. The settlement was moved to the mouth of the Suerre River due to scarcity of food and strong indigenous opposition. It was abandoned soon afterward. A number of subsequent expeditions organized in the seventeenth century met similar fates.

The Central Valley was not conquered easily either. The first expedition to penetrate the territory was that of Juan de Cavallón in 1561, which resulted in the foundation of the town of Castillo de Garcimuñoz, a settlement called Los Reyes and a port called Landecho. All these footholds, however, were extremely precarious due to opposition from the indigenous groups.

The real conqueror of the Central Valley was Juan Vázquez de Coronado, who after 1562 embarked on a mission to co-opt the *caciques* and lords. Oriented by this objective, the invading party explored the territory in detail and made efforts to forge alliances with different indigenous groups. In the process, Vázquez de Coronado founded Cartago, Costa Rica's colonial capital.

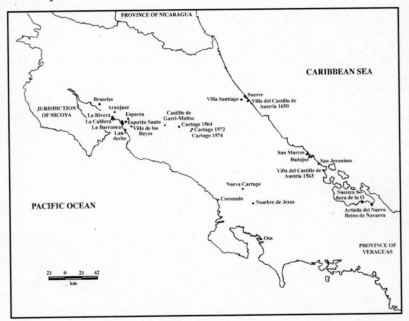

Spanish settlements, 16th century.

The use of persuasive tactics was not entirely successful. In 1564 Vázquez de Coronado faced a series of indigenous uprisings, and in putting them down he ordered the quartering of numerous rebels. The agitation

The greatest obstacle to the pacification of this province is a chief called Garabito... and he is not satisfied with having sacrificed a soldier taken from the party of Licenciado [Juan de] Cavallón... Instead he exhorts and even threatens all the others not to show due obèdience to Your Majesty or to recognize God the Father. For this I have subjected him to trial: he is condemned to death, and war shall be made upon him as if he had rebelled.

Juan Vázquez de Coronado, December 1562.

reached its climax in 1568, when Cartago was nearly abandoned, something avoided at the eleventh hour by the arrival of the governor, Perafán de Rivera with food and other help. After quelling the rebellion, the functionary of the Spanish Crown began to distribute *encomiendas* among the conquerors, entitling them to exact labor, services and a variety of products from the defeated indigenous groups.

Spanish control over the Central Valley was consolidated by the end of the sixteenth century. Aside from their technological advantages (the horse, metal and gunpowder), the conquerors took advantage of conflicts among indigenous groups, and co-opted their leaders as often as possible. The Spanish also benefitted from the disease,

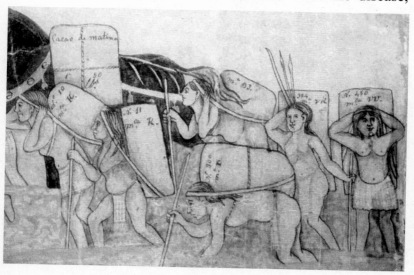

Exploitation of indigenous people.

exploitation and war that they had provoked. Despite this mayhem, the vanquished challenged their new masters militarily on many occasions, although the more common response was to escape to areas where the Spanish could not reach them, in the Caribbean jungles, in the plains of San Carlos and in Talamanca.

Bows and arrows against firearms.

At the beginning of the seventeenth century, Costa Rica was a poor, empty, isolated and marginal colony. For the most part, the territory was either unoccupied or populated by *indios bravos* ("wild Indians"). The principal settlement, situated in the Central Valley, was a tiny world surrounded by mountains, far from the coast and distant from the principal trade routes. The fact that the territory

The land is exhausted, and the city of Esparça totally depopulated... The natives perish and [their communities] disappear... These and many other problems... will cease should Your Majesty order this province joined to your royal audiencia of Panama...

Council of Cartago, April 1622.

was administratively part of the Kingdom of Guatemala made it easier for the merchants of the north to engage in speculation at the expense of the Spanish settlers of Cartago and their offspring. These new Costa Rican elites on the furthest periphery of the empire were *ultimus inter pares* (last among equals). Not surprisingly, they dreamed of uniting with the dynamic *Audiencia* of Panama, where the treasures of Peru were unloaded and carried across the isthmus to fleets bound for Spain. The dream, alas, did not come true.

CHAPTER 4

THE EARLY COLONIAL WORLD (1570-1700)

After 1570, Costa Rica participated in the colonial economy through trade in a wide variety of products. Among the foodstuffs exported from the territory were corn, honey, beans, salt, flour, corn biscuits, garlic and chickens. Artisanal products like ceramics, hammocks and blankets were also shipped out of Costa Rica. Primary materials gathered or produced for export included pearls; indigo and dyes made from shells; cotton thread; sisal, agave and other fibers for making cord and tackle; lard, beef jerky and livestock.

The goods ended up in any number of colonial centers. In Nicaragua, apart from Granada and Leon, they went to the port of El Realejo, the site of important shipyards. In the

Commerce.

south, they were destined for Panama, Nombre de Dios, Portobelo, Cartagena and Peru.

Imports were almost exclusively made up of manufactured items: textiles (fabrics and clothes), plates and cutlery, tools and a range of luxury articles. The principal overland route of trade and communication was the famous "camino real", opened in 1601: the road traversed the arduous terrain between Nicaragua and Cartago, passing through Guanacaste and Esparza.

Costa Rica had a number of ports. On the Caribbean, the port of Suerre functioned between 1576 and 1636; in the latter year Moín and Matina were made usable for docking and loading ships. On the Pacific coast the port of Caldera was established sometime during the 1570s, as were those of Abangares and Alvarado.

The dry coastal plains of the Pacific north-west had abundant, valuable hardwoods (cedar and pochote). From the sixteenth century onwards, this area had three shipyards: Nandayure in Nicoya, and Juan Solano and La Barranca further south near Esparza. Vessels of all kinds were built and repaired in the yards, which created a demand for skilled labor, foodstuffs, fabrics for sail-making, and fiber for ropes and rigging. The consumption of these items helped to give a certain dynamism to commerce in the early seventeenth century,

I also inform Your Majesty that together with a city of this province, a port has been founded which apparently is frequented by frigates which come from Panama for corn and honey and oils and sarsaparilla, and birds and wood, and horses and mules are shipped, and this place is called Esparza.

Alonso de Cubillo, Treasurer of Costa Rica, March 1580.

which was subsequently enhanced by an active mule trade.

Costa Rica's exports went through three basic cycles of expansion and decline in the seventeenth century. The first cycle was the raising of mules for export, which lasted from 1590 to 1680. The beasts of burden were raised in the Pacific plain of the entire Central American region, from Choluteca to Nicoya and Esparza. They were then rested and pastured in different parts of Costa Rica's Central Valley (Barva, Poás and Aserrí), prior to being shipped from Caldera to Panama, where they were put to work carrying cargo across the isthmus. After 1601, this ocean voyage was substituted by caravans that relied on exploiting the labor of the indigenous peoples of Quepos and Boruca.

Competition from other mule-raising areas in Nicaragua and Honduras put a dent in the Costa Rican industry, which switched to the export of lard and leather to Panama after 1650. The new trade was based on the exploitation of free-ranging herds of cattle, the beginning of a style of ranching based on the use of vast extensions of land that would come to characterize stock-raising in Guanacaste. However, the people of the area sacrificed cattle in excessive numbers, wasting milk and leaving meat to be devoured by vultures or to rot. The unregulated slaughter was so great that it came to threaten

Exporting mules.

They trade with Panama in tallow from the cattle in the valley of Bagaces ...From one cow they get two or three arrobas [about 11.5 kg] and they sell each one at eight reales in exchange for goods, so that their profit scarcely reaches three pesos, making the cow on the hoof [potentially] more valuable; but because they have no one to buy from them, the owners engage in sporadic slaughters with only the purpose of getting the small quantities of tallow they trade.

Governor Diego de la Haya Fernández, March 1719.

the very existence of these wild herds. The danger of extinction was only averted in the eighteenth century when the opening of the Guatemalan market to cattle on the hoof led the *hacendados* of Guanacaste and Esparza to manage the livestock more carefully.

The principal export cycle of Costa Rica in the century between 1650 and 1750 was that of cacao. Cultivation of the cocoa bean was stimulated by sale of the product in Nicaragua. The real boom period (1727-47), however, was a result of the opening of markets for

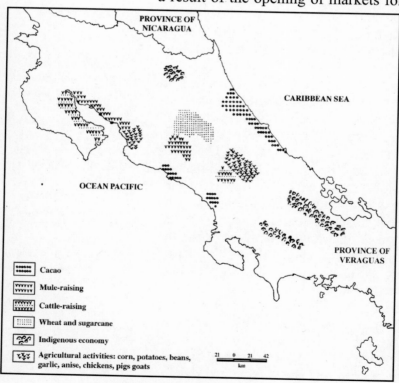

The Costa Rica economy of the 16th and 17th centuries.

the fruit in the principal centers of the Caribbean: Jamaica, Curaçao, Portobelo and Cartagena. Cocoa cultivation transformed the port of Matina into a center of contraband, especially with the English and the Dutch; it dynamized Costa Rica's colonial economy through trade, and also by giving it a curious monetary unit – the cacao *peso* (a certain amount of cocoa beans equalled one peso) – established in 1709 in the face of a grave shortage of silver.

The road to Matina.

The hope of securing a continuous, prosperous link with the established flows of colonial commerce was a vain one. The splendor of the cacao boom was fleeting, its rapid decline due to a combination of different factors: taxes imposed by the Crown, an absence of appropriate roads and ports, deficiencies in quality due to production methods, and attacks by pirates and the fearsome *zambos mosquitos* (a Caribbean ethnicity resulting from the union of indigenous people and marooned slaves).

The most important reason for the decline of Costa Rica's cacao boom, however, was competition from other, more potent areas of the colonial world like Caracas, Maracaibo and Guayaquil. Cocoa cultivation continued, and it picked up considerably at the end of the eighteenth century when demand rose in Cartagena, but this boom was even more short-lived than the first, lasting no more than a decade (1770-80).

These diverse commercial activities were made possible by the exploitation of indigenous and black labor. In 1569, the governor, Perafán de Rivera had formally distributed the right to exploit the indigenous peoples, known as *encomienda*: 85 conquistadors were assigned 208 settlements containing some 22,000 people; at the same time, the Crown was allotted exclusive tribute rights over three towns (Pacaca, Quepo and Chome) containing 2,700 people. *Encomenderos* were obliged to evangelize their subjects; in exchange, they received free labor for their lands and their households, and considerable quantities of corn, beans, fibers, wax, honey, salt and other such products.

I [the governor] *order the said Indians to provide their encomendero... twenty-five hanegas [1.6 bushels] of corn... and to give him one hundred and thirteen arrobas of sisal and twelve Peruvian jars of honey, and nine arrobas of wax, and three hundred new blankets... and six arrobas of pita rope... and that they sow for him a field of beans... and that they give him immediately one hundred jugs and one hundred pots... and six Indian men and two Indian women for* [collecting] *firewood, herbage and to grind and serve in his house...*

From the town of Ciruro, made up of 300 indigenous tributaries, for the *encomendero* Matías Palacios, 1569.

As the total number of natives declined, the exploitation of the remaining ones intensified, particularly towards the end of the sixteenth century. The constant drop in the potential resources that could be demanded of an ever smaller group of Indians sharpened the conflict between the local representatives of the Crown, those of the Church and the *encomenderos*, since none wished to cede the right to maximize their exploitation of the indigenous people. The result of this intensified exploitation was statistically evident in the 1611 report of a colonial functionary who visited Costa Rica. He calculated that the total number of natives in *encomienda* was a little over 7,000, or 67 percent less than the number distributed in 1569. In the face of this crisis, the Spaniards became more anxious than ever to conquer the areas occupied by the *indios bravos*, the territory of Talamanca in particular.

The effort to subdue the natives on the Caribbean side, those in the Pacific south and those on the northern plains was a drawn-out process with mixed results. Military expeditions alternated with the attempts of missionaries to pacify areas through the conquest of souls, and with the creation of temporary bases for capturing natives who could be resettled (and so exploited) in zones under Spanish control. The most intense period of such expeditions was the century from 1611 to 1709.

The indigenous groups of these areas offered fierce resistance. Expeditions dropped off after 1709, the year that the *indios bravos* of Talamanca launched a rebellion. In 1710, after the revolt was put down, the Spanish began reprisals with financial and military assistance from Guatemala; the repression culminated with the capture and execution of the leader of the uprising, the *cacique*, Pablo Presbere.

The Spanish had to explore other options for augmenting their labor supply. The principal one was to import black slaves, often in the context of flourishing contraband. The slave

I sentence the said Pablo Presbere... to be... placed on a pack animal and carried through the streets of this city [Cartago]... *and outside its walls, to be tied to a post and blindfolded... whereupon he shall be shot with a cross-bow... and later... his head shall be cut off and placed high upon... that same post...*

Governor Lorenzo Antonio de Granda y Balbín, July 1710.

traffic, closely linked with cacao commerce, was most active in the years between 1690 and 1730. Not coincidentally, 1690 was the year of a major epidemic that decimated the indigenous population in the Central Valley; in its wake, the governor prohibited the labor of natives from Talamanca in the cacao-growing areas of Matina, motivating growers to look to the slave markets of the Caribbean.

The execution of Presbere in 1710.

Slaves resisted their lot in a variety of ways, mostly through subtle forms of subverting the master's will rather than through overt opposition. Their labor was exploited fairly cautiously in Costa Rica, given that the elevated cost of a slave made him or her an investment that had to be protected by the owner. Slavery in Cartago and Matina was much less brutal than it was in other colonial areas, the plantations of Brazil and the Caribbean islands in particular.

The slaves themselves had a variety of opportunities for purchasing their liberty. They might also be manumitted (given their freedom), sometimes a recognition of services written into the will of the master, other times because they were the child of the master, or the mother of his child. At the very least, 430 slaves purchased their freedom or were manumitted between 1648 and 1824. Free blacks and mulattos were particularly visible in the Pacific north where they often worked as overseers on the vast cattle ranches. Over time, black people whose ancestors had come to Costa Rica as slaves were ethnically and socially incorporated through *mestizaje* (racial mixture).

My father-in-law, Seferino Luna... was married to my mother-in-law, Dominga Solano, both of them slaves, and... with their labor they were able to buy their freedom and afterwards they had two free children, one of whom is my wife...

Antonio Calderón, a peasant from Cartago, July 1822.

The beginnings of San José.

On a very agreeable plain... there are two hundred and twenty houses with tiled roof and one hundred and ninety-four with straw roof, farms dedicated to milling sugar, others to raising cattle, and others to growing wheat, corn, tobacco, beans, onions, garlic, anise, coriander and dill...

San José, according to Bishop Pedro Agustín Morel de Santa Cruz, September 1752.

The period from 1690 to 1750 saw the definitive decline of *encomienda* and slavery. The indigenous population had continued to fall, the *indios bravos* were unconquerable, and the end of the cacao boom also ended the thirst for more labor power. The elites of the era – the principal families of Cartago who traced their lineage to the conquerors – successfully controlled the ranches of Guanacaste and the cacao-growing areas of Matina. They monopolized wholesale and retail trade, and they dominated civil, military and ecclesiastical posts. Despite this, they had failed to construct a stable society based on the exploitation of an indigenous or black labor force.

The eighteenth century was a period of increasing racial mixture, marked by the rise of a free peasantry made up of these mestizos and of whites who were the descendants of impoverished *encomenderos*. These agricultural producers began to populate other parts of the Central Valley, in particular the fertile lands around San José, Heredia and Alajuela.

CHAPTER 5

MERCHANTS AND PEASANTS (1700-1850)

Over the course of the eighteenth century, Costa Rica was transformed by the expansion of peasant agriculture. Population growth around the colonial capital, Cartago, coincided with the exhaustion of available farm land. New generations of peasants had to look elsewhere, and they began the arduous task of settling the western side of the Central Valley. The expansion of the agricultural frontier led to the founding of new towns: Heredia in 1706, San José in 1736 and Alajuela in 1782.

The newly-settled areas did not have marked social inequalities at the outset. Still, in contrast to the myth that Costa Rica was a classless rural democracy in the late colonial period, certain differences were visible even among peasants and farmers. At the

Grinding rice or coffee by hand.

high end were those farmers who owned their own lands; at the low end were those peasants who farmed common lands provisionally made available to them. Some farms had a good deal more livestock than others. These differences in prosperity also determined the capacity of producers to acquire new technologies.

There shall be a commissioner to regulate the extraction of firewood and other materials from the mountain... and he must ensure that no one person strips or fells more than four trees... Among those who work on the edge of the mountain, each individual shall plant a tree at precise intervals of four varas [2.8 feet]...

Dispositions of the peasant owners of the mountain of Candelaria, San José, June 1845.

The basic unit of this agricultural world was the *chácara*, or family farm dedicated to varying combinations of subsistence and commercial agriculture (especially sugar cane), the raising of cattle, pigs and fowl, and crafts. The larger village community defined how land was to be used, how the forests were to be exploited (for firewood and for building materials), how water resources could be accessed, and so on. Apart from overseeing the commonwealth, village society regulated the everyday life of the peasant families, their values and world-views. The legal formulation and enforcement of their own rules gave these communities, already at the close of the colonial period, some self-government, and provided legal channels for resolving individual and collective conflicts.

The rural domains contrasted with the town centers of Cartago, San José, Heredia and Alajuela. Although tiny by urban standards, they differed from the rural world because they served as bases of specialized craft production and as sites of the homes of the most powerful and prosperous families. These principal *vecinos* maintained their preeminence in a variety of ways. They occupied civil, ecclesiastical and military positions. They monopolized the circulation of money and they acquired the right to collect the tithe (raking off a percentage in return for the service). They rented parcels of land to poor peasants, maintained large haciendas in Guanacaste and cacao growing areas on the Caribbean, owned slaves and ships, and controlled exports and imports.

Market day in Cartago.

Their wealth came mainly from commerce, which depended on their engaging in unequal exchange with the peasantry. Merchants acquired the surplus (what was left over after subsistence needs were met) from agriculture, from stock-raising or from craft production at less than its potential market value; they then exported it, usually to Nicaragua or to Panama. With the proceeds from their sales on these distant markets Costa Rica's merchants purchased manufactured goods, which they then imported and sold at inflated prices to the peasants and artisans of the Central Valley.

By the eighteenth century, the merchants lacked the means to extract goods and services systematically on the basis of ethnic difference, or through the use of force. As a result, exploitation in Costa Rica's Central Valley assumed the form of a basic mercantile link between two social groups who, although both juridically free, had different economic statures which allowed the merchant group to "buy low and sell high". This system of unequal exchange was reproduced one step up the ladder, between Costa Rican merchants and their foreign suppliers who were better situated in the hierarchy of colonial commerce.

As a result, the merchants of Guatemala, Nicaragua and Panama could fix advantageous terms for their purchase of the goods offered to them by Costa Rican merchants. They could also get away with a significant markup on manufactured wares. The merchants of the Central Valley, however, were not exploited as such. It would be more accurate to say that they were

A peasant.

incapable of retaining for themselves all the fruits of their exploitation of the peasantry and the artisans. Still, once he ventured outside the territory, the local merchant was at the mercy of his foreign trading partner, just as inside Costa Rica the peasant or artisan was at the mercy of the local merchant.

Because these merchants had no choice but to meet the prices of their foreign suppliers, imported articles were dear. Prices could not be raised excessively, though, since peasants always had the option not to buy at all. As a result, the largest share of merchants' profits depended on the extremely low price they paid for the produce of the land, or for goods coming from the family workshop. The *chácara* was not overly beholden to the laws of this market because it sold only that portion of produce that was left over after the needs of the household had been satisfied. Since agriculture and crafts relied by and large on family labor, the farm could still make a "profit" from the sale of its surplus, even if the price offered by the merchant was extremely low.

In the eighteenth century a new dynasty was installed on the Spanish throne. The Bourbon monarchy, influenced by the ideas of rational administration in vogue north of the Pyrenees, began a series of reforms intended to stimulate colonial commerce and so, by extension, raise the taxation revenues

They propose, then, to subject unfortunate Costa Ricans to going... all the way to Guatemala to purchase the materials they need, or at least as far as Leon... to buy the same goods already marked up... The demand [of the Guatemalan merchants to prohibit Costa Rican trade with Panama] *is selfish, unjust, oppressive and unacceptable...*

Complaint of the merchants of the Central Valley, August 1813.

of the Crown. The economy of Costa Rica's Central Valley was affected by these reforms, which included the creation of a state monopoly over the production and sale of tobacco and alcohol.

The regulated sale of liquor increased. Although this commerce was confined to the local market, it spurred the cultivation of sugar cane and the manufacture of *trapiches* (small sugar mills). Tobacco cultivation was stimulated first by market demand in Nicaragua, but production expanded considerably between 1787 and 1792 when the colonial authorities in Guatemala granted Costa Rica the tobacco monopoly for all Central America (it fell off just as quickly once the privilege was eliminated).

Most of the commercial expansion in sugarcane and tobacco cultivation

Trapiche (sugar mill).

took place on the western side of the Central Valley. This was due to the fact that, in contrast to the peasants around Cartago, those in the new areas of settlement were more prosperous and so could invest in land, in livestock and in new technologies. Between 1750 and 1790, economic and population growth shifted away from the old colonial capital and towards Heredia, San José and Alajuela. San José soon outgrew Heredia and Alajuela, largely because tobacco production was concentrated there, and because its farmers had privileged access to the credit of the new administrative entity established there to oversee the monopoly, the *Factoría de Tabacos*.

By 1800, the Central Valley already accounted for the overwhelming majority of Costa Rica's population. Of the province's 50,000 people, over 80 percent lived in this series of intramontane basins. Six out of every ten were mestizos. Whites (Spaniards or their ancestors who claimed to have no mixed blood) accounted for 6 to 9 percent. After experiencing a resurgence in the second half of the eighteenth century, indigenous people made up 14 percent of those who dwelled in the province (half of these lived in the plains of San Carlos, Sarapiquí and Talamanca). A small black populace, one percent of the total, was concentrated around Cartago and Matina. *Pardos*, mulattos and *zambos* (mixed

In a short period of time ...I have seen a large number of good houses erected [in San José], *and those who inhabit them appear out of nowhere. Every day families arrive from other places... to establish residence in this* [city], *lured by the fortunes that flow from the* [tobacco] *harvests that are the envy of neighboring areas...*

Mariano Montealegre, Administrator of the Royal Tobacco Monopoly, 1818.

race people with markedly black descent) predominated in Guanacaste,
and accounted for 17 percent of the
total populace.

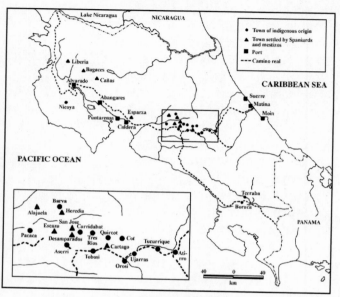

Settlements, ports and roads of Costa Rica, 1750-1821.

The territory as a whole hosted a
variety of economic and social struc-
tures. Itinerant agriculture was practiced by the indigenous cultures of the
outlying regions on the northern plains
and in Talamanca. Though in decline
by the end of the eighteenth century,
the cacao-growing areas of the Caribbean coast were characterized by
slave labor. In Esparza and Guanacaste a free peasantry, occupied as much
in hunting as in horticulture, provided
occasional labor for the haciendas.
These centers of live-stock raising on

the Pacific plains benefitted from the expansion of indigo production in Guatemala and El Salvador after 1750, when Europe's industrial revolution stimulated demand for the dye. The displacement of pasturage by indigo plants opened a market for cattle on the hoof, which was raised by the ranchers of the provinces and then driven north.

The Central Valley was economically and socially the most important region of Costa Rica, however. Its economy was based on peasant production, essentially devoid of servitude, and it was an ethnically and culturally integrated area. Mestizos provided the social ballast, and they shared a strong Catholic and Hispanic culture with the elites. True, in the

The estate of Don Juan [José Bonilla, located in Guanacaste] covered as much ground as a German principality, containing two hundred thousand acres... A small portion of it was cultivated... the rest was a roaming ground for cattle. More than ten thousand animals were wandering over it, almost as wild as the deer...

John Lloyd Stephens, traveller and diplomat from the United States, 1840.

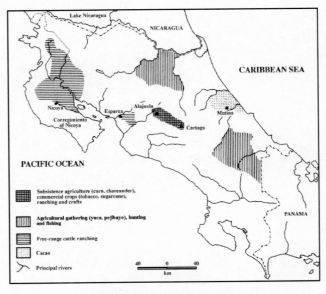

Economic zones of Costa Rica, 1750-1821.

houses of the rich it was common to see icons or the frames of religious paintings made of gold or silver, and occasionally inlaid with precious stones, while in the huts of the poor simple engravings in paper were the norm. But the same saints were worshipped in the household of merchant, artisan and peasant alike, and all held similar beliefs about sin, marriage and death.

This world began to change after 1821, when Spanish colonial authority was overthrown in Mexico, and Central America suddenly found itself independent. Free trade, the arrival of foreign entrepreneurs, a small mining boom and the harvesting of Brazil wood all helped to accelerate economic growth. Momentous political and cultural changes followed hard on the heels of these new contacts with the world market.

Mining operations, with their epicenter in Montes de Aguacate, flourished between 1821 and 1843. In 1828, during the first flush of the fever, the Casa de Moneda (the mint) was established in San José. Because it created a demand for labor and supplies from the Central Valley, this mining cycle gave a boost to the internal market as well as helping to monetize an economy that had long suffered from a shortage of metal currency. Nevertheless, the boom was not nearly as lucrative as had been hoped.

Holy Week in San José, 1858.

Brazilwood, valued for its dye, grew wild in the forests of the Pacific coast of Central America. Between 1800 and 1840, it was an important export product, with the trade reaching its peak in the 1830s. Purchased by English importers in particular, the timber briefly served as a source of capital accumulation for the merchants of the Central Valley. Costa Rica's clusters of Brazil trees, however, were much scarcer than those of Nicaragua. The easily accessible stands were rapidly exhausted, and the surviving trees, situated at ever greater distances from the beaches, were less and less attractive because of the difficulties of harvesting and hauling them.

The desire to find a stable link with the world market was only fulfilled with coffee. The "golden bean" experienced a period of dramatic expansion after 1830, with cultivation initially concentrated almost exclusively in and around San José. The fruit was exported to Chile first, and was then shipped around the Horn and north to the rapidly growing British market. Coffee exports consolidated Costa Rica's foreign commerce: their volume rose from a little over 8,000 quintals in 1840 to almost 100,000 quintals in 1848. Coffee farming, stimulated by cheap and ever more available credit, transformed agriculture into capitalist enterprise, fomenting

Having arrived on the coast of Nicoya with the object of loading Brazilwood aboard an English frigate... [I have] been charged with the clandestine introduction of goods, and for not having paid Docking and Tonnage fees in Puntarenas...

Fate of the English Captain, Walter Bridge, September 1829.

privatization of the land and the creation of a market in wage labor.

The merchant families of the late colonial period now converted themselves into the principal *cafetaleros* of the nineteenth century. Their new form of domination was based on a triple control. First, they monopolized credit, especially the annual loans to finance the coffee harvest, but also credit for everyday purchases or long-term investment. Second, they dominated

El Laberinto (The Labyrinth), a coffee estate near San José.

the import and the export trade of Costa Rica. Third, they controlled the young industry's principal technology, constructing *beneficios* (processing facilities) that used the superior "wet method" for stripping the fruit of its skin, pulp and husk, and providing the seed – the coffee bean – its basic look and its base flavor. The first *beneficio* was built in 1838 by an immigrant from Catalonia, Buenaventura Espinach. Beneficios soon became strategic points of *cafetalero* control over the industry, as well as symbols of that domination.

This early agrarian capitalism in the Central Valley was shaped by peasant agriculture in important ways, however. The actual growing of coffee flourished on family farms, usually of less than twenty acres. As a result, the transition to agrarian capitalism in the Central Valley was characterized by strong pressures from below. The balance of social forces which had taken shape across the eighteenth century made it impossible for the new coffee bourgeoisie to expropriate the peasants violently or to submit them to servitude as occurred in the coffee industries of many other countries. The only option left open to the wealthy was to exercise a type of domination that recognized the liberty and the property of their social inferiors.

Non-violent resistance to agrarian capitalism came from some peasant families, often those too poor to be able to invest in coffee production. The rural poor used a variety of legal means to delay the privatization of communal lands. At the same time, the existence of abundant virgin land on the agricultural frontier gave poor or young peasants a chance to pioneer new areas, when land in their birthplace became

As soon as the crimson colour assumed by the ripe fruit indicates the time for cropping, numbers of men, women, and children are sent to gather the berry, which is piled in large heaps to soften the pulp for forty-eight hours, and then placed in tanks through which a large stream of water passes, where it is constantly stirred to free it from the outer pulp; after which it is spread out upon a platform, with which every coffee estate is furnished, to dry in the sun; but there still exists an inner husk, which, when perfectly dry, is, in the smaller estates, removed by treading the berry under the feet of oxen; and, in the larger, by water mills, which bruise the berry slightly to break the husk, and afterwards separate it by fanners.

Robert Glasgow Dunlop, Scottish traveller, 1844.

The same owners of small plots, after finishing their reduced labors, are employed to work on the big haciendas, or find work using their ox carts or mules to transport the berries...

Francisco Solano Astaburuaga, Chilean diplomat, 1857.

too expensive due to coffee expansion. This pattern of migration among the lower classes of a small population limited the pool of wage labor available for the coffee harvest, and so coffee pickers had to be attracted through higher wages. The dynamic gave peasants a chance to maintain access to land, and so delayed the emergence of a large landless class of rural laborers.

Creating an appropriate political system for this newly independent society and this new export economy was not a straightforward matter. The 1812 Constitution of Cadiz, approved in the context of Napoleon's invasion of the Iberian Peninsula, fomented the expansion of the *cabildos*, or town councils, throughout Spanish America. As a result, on the eve of independence, Costa Rica was characterized by a fragmented sovereignty expressed in the various cabildos, dominated by the leading merchants and officials. This arrangement reinforced local identities. At the time of independence in 1821 Costa Rica was not so much a country as it was a territory ruled by four affiliated but rival towns: Cartago, Heredia, San José and Alajuela.

Each town had its own plan for meeting the brave new world. Initially the most obvious course was to adhere to the Mexican Empire, which sent an army to conquer those parts of Central America that did not submit willingly.

The cities of Cartago and Heredia favored annexation, while San José and Alajuela opposed it, preferring some form of republican independence. This conflict culminated in the first civil war: the battle of Ochomogo of April 5th, 1823. After Cartago's defeat, San José became the capital of Costa Rica.

The *cabildo* of Cartago.

As it was, Mexico's imperial dreams collapsed in 1823, while efforts to create a Central American federal republic came to fruition. Costa Rica participated in this federal experiment for most of the latter's troubled existence (1823-40), sending funds, assuming a portion of the debt, and electing representatives to the distant Congress. However, the fate of the Central American republic would be decided by events in Guatemala and El Salvador. On the margins of those deep divisions and disputes,

Costa Ricans were left to sort out their own internal affairs.

The battle of Ochomogo was followed by twelve years of peace. However, in 1835 local rivalries burst into a second civil conflict (the War of the League). San José defeated the alliance formed by Cartago, Heredia and Alajuela and consolidated its position as head of the country. The capital of agrarian capitalism was also the

Principal barracks of San José, 1858.

capital of the State of Costa Rica, and then of the Republic of Costa Rica, proclaimed in 1848 when the project to create a Central American federation had clearly failed.

The growing political instability after 1835 gave rise to the country's first dictatorship, led by Braulio Carrillo (1838-42), which combined privatization of the lands with persecution of vagrancy, and the strengthening of central government with the weakening of Church and municipalities. Henceforth, the struggle among the major towns over which one would be the capital was displaced by the competition between political factions to win control of the executive branch.

Despite these early conflicts, Costa Rica was fortunate to avoid the prolonged civil wars that set back so many Latin American countries after independence. Of particular importance in this regard, the brief and sporadic battles between the rival towns of the Central Valley did not encourage professionalization of the armed forces. In any case, the country's early economic expansion (especially coffee) offered greater opportunities for social ascent than did military prowess, and an abundance of agricultural opportunities also limited the growth of a bureaucratic elite.

The young country had mixed luck in its external affairs. Costa Rica consolidated its sovereignty over Guanacaste in 1824 when the people of Nicoya decided in favor of annexation to Costa Rica rather than to war-torn Nicaragua. On the southern frontier, however, Bocas del Toro was lost to Colombian expansionism in 1836 (present-day Panama was then part of

Our militia is a collection of honorable citizens: peaceful farmers, artisans and laborers who devote themselves with honesty and constancy to their private occupations, live from their industry and have no aspirations beyond those of fulfilling their domestic obligations and defending the State when the law summons them...

Juan Mora Fernández, Head of State, 1829.

Colombia). In 1841, the Costa Rican government was capable of a show of strength on the Caribbean side, suspending payment of its annual tribute to the British-backed *zambos mosquitos* (the payment, begun in 1779, was so that they would not attack Matina). Finally, Costa Rica negotiated the erection of its own diocese in 1850, thus ending subordination to the bishopric of Leon in Nicaragua.

Cathedral of San José, 1858.

The country's principal diplomatic success was avoiding involvement in the horrendous civil wars that marked the woeful history of the Central American Federal Republic. Costa Rica was affected by the aftermath of those civil wars, however. Following the decisive defeat of federalist forces in Guatemala in 1840, their leader, General Francisco

Morazán disembarked in Caldera in April of 1842 with an army. He was supported by local officers supposedly loyal to Carrillo. Carrillo was obliged to go into exile (he was murdered in El Salvador in 1845).

Designated provisional Head of State, Morazán tried to convert Costa Rica into the political and military staging ground for a new campaign to unite Central America. The attempt ended in September of 1842 with a violent outburst from the plebeians of San José. They overthrew the great *caudillo* with the assistance of disgruntled members of the local elite, and later insisted that Morazán be executed (he was, by firing squad, in the south-west corner of what is now the Central Park of San José).

In the three decades after 1821, central power tended to become stronger.

On Sunday the 14th of September cries of 'Long live sacred liberty!', 'Long live our father San José!', 'Long live our lady of Los Angeles!', and 'Long live the united towns!' could be heard everywhere. The exact strength of the people in arms is not easy to calculate; but it can be safely deduced that, counting those armed with clubs, machetes, rifles and rocks, [and including] women, the number surpassed 5,000. Officers were scarce, and they were barely necessary...

Chronicle of the popular revolt that overthrew Morazán in September 1842.

Morazán disembarks in Costa Rica, 1842.

[T]*oday he* [the husband] *has beaten her, insulted her and mopped the floor with her calling her a whore and streetwalker because earlier this week the husband left one* real *tied in this handkerchief which she claims to have spent on candles and lard, and as he did not find it today, he has done what she says...*

Manuela Cordero versus her husband, Vicente Montero in the Court of San José, May 1844.

Especially important was the expansion of a network of civil tribunals that soon began to displace the Church and the village communities in the channeling of a variety of disputes, from matters relating to the privatization of land to those of family life (notably, women began to use these courts to bring charges of domestic violence). Aside from reinforcing the tendency to deal with conflict through legal forms, this change helped to legitimize the new republican institutions and deepen the secularization of society.

Centralization of political power happened together with a change in the franchise. After independence, Costa Rican legislation had followed the path established in the Constitution of Cadiz in granting electoral rights to the great majority of adult males. Elections were indirect and happened in three stages. First, citizens selected electors, then electors chose delegates and finally these delegates picked the Head of State and the deputies.

In 1825 the Congress approved economic restrictions for being an elector, which were strengthened by the Carrillo regime in 1841. After the overthrow of Morazán, a new Constitution (1844) introduced the direct vote and restricted citizenship according to personal fortune (200 pesos minimum). The failure of this experience led in 1847 to the return to an indirect system of two stages, which was in effect until 1913.

The restrictions on citizenship disappeared, but the requirements for electors were maintained and increased (from now on literacy would be mandatory). However, political exclusion was soon reintroduced. In 1848, the very Constitution that finally declared Costa Rica a republic stripped thousands of Costa Ricans of their citizenship, and blocked many others from running as electors.

Tensions produced by this political development were sharpened by a growing division between city and countryside. The leadership of San José, decisive in determining the course of Costa Rica's development, was expressed in a buoyant urban culture. By the 1850s coffee wealth had Europeanized consumer tastes in clothing, food and books. It was also behind a diversification of entertainment. One could now attend classes in languages, in dance and in a variety of specialized skills, discuss business over a game of billiards, place bets at the cockfight, and enjoy Shakespeare and operetta at the new Teatro Mora. The city also experienced growth in infrastructure and services, with the appearance of two-story buildings, street-lamps and pavement, cabs, pharmacies and stores. Later in the century, bourgeois prosperity and taste would find their maximum expression in the European

Gustavo ad Meinecke, Offers at reasonable prices. The best Wines and Liquors as well as Westphalia Ham, Meats, Patés, Legumes, Dutch and Lymbury fresh Cheeses, Saltfish or fish preserved in oil, Fruits in syrup and cognac, Olives, pickles, Mustard, Sauces and sundries.

Advertisement in the newspaper, *Álbum Semanal*, 24 April 1858.

Cockfight in San José, 1858.

eclecticism of the National Theater, Costa Rica's temple of civilization and progress, which was inaugurated in 1897 with a performance of Gounod's opera, *Faust* (preceded by the strains of the Costa Rican national anthem and the *Marseillaise*).

The urbanity of the principal towns, and especially of the capital city, was associated with an expansion of print culture. The first printing press was brought to Costa Rica in 1830, and between that year and 1849 some 17 newspapers and over 100 books and pamphlets were published in the country. Municipal governments sponsored education, though poor towns provided less schooling, and poor families were less likely to send children to school. Nevertheless, the community of readers did broaden and diversify. This process was promoted by the growth of the Casa de Enseñanza de Santo Tomás, opened as a general school in San José in 1814. By the time it was converted into a University in 1843, the works of Adam Smith, Jeremy Bentham and Eugène Sue were circulating through the upper echelons of society.

Teatro Nacional, San José, 1909.

These new European dispositions of Costa Rica's coffee elite were promoted by the influence of immigrants from the Old World. Costa Rican society experienced an early process of secularization, which was most visible in the behaviors, attitudes and tastes of the wealthy. Politicians and professionals enthusiastically embraced the Enlightenment, Liberalism, Masonry and the ideology of progress (in its capitalist rather than socialist version).

In marked contrast to this modernist impulse, peasants and artisans remained faithful to local identities based on village or town traditions, with deep Catholic and colonial roots. This cultural separation underlay a growing social tension, one that became sharper over the second half of the nineteenth century.

The *Zapatería Francesa*, a shoeshop in San José, 1858.

CHAPTER 6

COFFEE, CAPITALISM AND THE LIBERAL STATE (1850-1890)

Early in the new year of 1840 an adventurer and diplomat from the United States, John Lloyd Stephens approached San José on muleback. Having recently traversed war-torn Guatemala and El Salvador he was amazed to find social peace, and vast expanses of land planted in regimented rows of coffee trees. The stunning take-off in Costa Rica's coffee industry was stimulated by the high prices that prevailed throughout the nineteenth century, despite short periods of crisis. Cultivation of the "golden bean", initially concentrated around San José, extended to Cartago, Heredia and Alajuela after 1850.

The colonization of the agricultural frontier carried coffee even further afield. From 1830 onwards, young

Picking coffee in Tres Ríos, Cartago, 1920.

peasant couples set off to conquer virgin lands. The western portion of the Central Valley (from Alajuela to San Ramón) was the axis of that displacement, and coffee was planted in their pioneering footsteps from 1860 onwards. Thirty years later, coffee flourished in the valleys of the Reventazón and Turrialba, thanks to the completion of the Atlantic Railway. By 1930 coffee was being planted in San Carlos to the north, in Nicoya on the Pacific, and to the south in Tarrazú, though the bulk of the harvest continued to come from San José and environs.

Coffee was an injection of progress into the social and economic life of Costa Rica. Coffee wealth allowed the

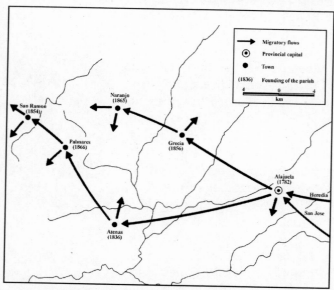

Settlement of the western Central Valley, 1782-1866.

import of fashionable goods and useful technologies, the opening of new roads and the improvement of old ones (in particular, that which linked San José to the Pacific coast), and the diversification of the internal market. The crop enriched a broad spectrum of small and middling farmers who, on top of a small parcel of land planted in coffee, prospered with the sale of foodstuffs and with the transport of coffee from the Central Valley to Puntarenas, which grew into a bustling port town thanks to the dizzying expansion of the country's international trade.

Carretas (ox carts).

The social and political effects of the coffee boom were visible early on. The losers in this process were poor peasants, hurt by the privatization of common lands, and indigenous communities of the Central Valley, dispossessed of their lands by the feverish pace of agricultural colonization. The only option for the native groups was to move ever further into the wilderness (towards Talamanca, for the most part), a process that condemned them to marginalization, poverty and neglect. The destiny of poor peasants was wage labor. The proportion of agricultural wage laborers in the Economically Active Population rose from 25 percent in 1864 to 36 percent in 1892, and reached 40 percent in 1927.

At the apex of the social pyramid, elites found in coffee an early source of stability and wealth that consolidated

[We denounce] *the abuses and excesses committed in the guise of legality against the simple class... in order to favor with land that belongs to us by legitimate title – title that we have justified with the sweat of our brow – persons associated with the Administration, continuous leeching by the treasury, speculators in the calamities that befall the poor class, and the friends and family of don Juan Rafael Mora who appropriated the largest part without shame.*

Protest of the peasants of Turrúcares, Alajuela, May 1860.

*Every day one sees
businesses fail, dis-
trains, sales of farms at
minimal prices, and
most people feel the
need to cease cultivat-
ing* [coffee] *because instead of profits it only
leaves them with losses.*

José María Castro, President
of the Republic, April 1849.

Juan Rafael Mora Porras. Oil
on canvas. Tomás Povedano,
1925.

their power. For those who weathered
the economic crisis of 1847-49
brought on by a sharp drop in the international price of coffee, the future
looked bright indeed. With its almost
100,000 inhabitants, the society was
ever more complex and diverse, but at
the same time more integrated and
economically dynamic. Agricultural
colonization replaced jungles and
forests with planted fields and active
pastures, while San José lost its village
look as it became wealthy enough to
dress itself in city finery.

The near future, however, was to
be tragic. In 1854, in the heat of Nicaragua's civil war, one of the factions
contracted the services of William
Walker, a mercenary (or "filibuster", in
the parlance of the time) from the United States. Arriving in 1855, Walker
soon took over Nicaragua. Although it
is often affirmed that his interest from
the beginning was to make Central
America a slave republic, Walker's im-
mediate objective was to dominate the
south of Nicaragua and the north of
Costa Rica. This territory was considered strategically vital for the construction of an inter-oceanic canal using the
San Juan River and Lake Nicaragua
(long considered an excellent alternative to Panama). The President of Costa
Rica, Juan Rafael Mora (1849-59) ap-
pealed to the governments and peoples
of Central America to combine forces
and drive Walker from the region.

Mora supplemented Costa Rica's small regular army with peasant and artisan militias, and rode north to meet the enemy. A Costa Rican victory at Santa Rosa, Guanacaste in March of 1856 was followed by the defeat of Walker's main army at Rivas on 11 April. In the last days of December, assistance from the British allowed the Costa Ricans to seize control of the San Juan River, thus depriving Walker of any reinforcements and supplies. The US adventurer finally surrendered to the Central American armies on 1 May 1857 (following further incursions in subsequent years, Walker was finally executed in 1860 by firing squad in the Honduran port of Trujillo).

The Burning of the Mesón. Oil on canvas. Enrique Echandi, 1896. The representation of Juan Santamaría as a mulatto peasant scandalized fin-de-siècle Liberals.

The worst of the fighting had fallen to Costa Rica. After the victory at Rivas in 1856, cholera was brought back by the troops and took the lives of almost one-tenth of the populace. This, and the enormous expense of the war, helped to sink the country into economic recession. Between 1856 and 1858 the coffee sector was badly affected by the shortage of laborers and the contraction of credit resulting from the war, and the economy did not show signs of recovery until 1859.

Costa Ricans had paid a terrible price to protect their young republic. That heroic sacrifice would come to be symbolized by the figure of Juan Santamaría, a humble laborer from Alajuela whose voluntary act of courage, though resulting in his own death, had turned the tide of the battle of Rivas in favor of the Costa Rican troops. Santamaría was reported to have set fire to a building from where Walker's army was decimating Costa Rican troops with rifle fire.

The so-called "National Campaign" of 1856-57 had a bloody epilogue: President Mora was deposed in a coup in 1859, and subsequently shot in 1860 as he tried to return to the country and take power again. Although the execution was exceptional, this was another in a long line of struggles between competing coffee clans who, between 1840 and 1870, intermittently deposed one another through

We had undertaken our operation to put [the mesón] *to the torch, when I directed my gaze towards Santamaría and saw that he turned sideways... and fell to one side, closing his eyes at the same time, I also noted that the burning bits falling from the eaves had lit his hair on fire, I saw the blood flow around his neck and I knew that he was dead.*

Gerónimo Segura, veteran of the National Campaign, August 1891.

barracks coups in order to gain direct access to the spoils of power. As the country became more complex in every way, such amateur, clannish government was no longer capable of providing coherence and direction to national development.

The transformation of politics began in 1870 under the dictatorship of General Tomás Guardia (1870-82). Although authoritarian in character, the two decades of rule by Guardia and his successors, Próspero Fernández (1882-85) and Bernardo Soto (1885-89), saw the expansion of public administration, and the rise of a group of politicians and intellectuals who had a clear plan of reform. Their goal was to create a modern state and society. These men were known as "the Olympians" because of the arrogance they displayed in dictating their Liberal reforms during the 1880s.

Like similar efforts throughout Latin America at this time, Costa Rica's reforms were intended to strengthen political authority, favor the expansion of capitalist agriculture, and "civilize" the lower classes. New civil and penal codes were enacted, and police and administrative posts were multiplied throughout the country. The state inaugurated civil registries of births, deaths and marriages. Of most importance, a centralized, secular, and free system of primary education was created (and made mandatory) to instruct the

The life of every inhabitant of Costa Rica is inviolable.

Tomás Guardia October 18, 1877.

Tomás Guardia Gutiérrez. Oil on canvas. A. Esttagny, no date.

The great risk [parents] *run of endangering their eternal salvation should they surrender their children to unbelieving male and female teachers, who for that very reason are immoral...*

Warning of the Costa Rican clergy, 1881.

uncouth children of artisans, laborers and peasants of the country in new skills and new values. The result of this effort was most notable in drastic increases in literacy: by the 1920s 87 percent of city residents, two-thirds of townspeople, and 58 percent of rural folk over 9 years of age could read and write.

With messianic zeal, the priests of progress – lawyers, physicians, teachers and journalists – began to spread the modern values of patriotism, capitalism, science, hygiene and racial purity. They encouraged their flock to perceive the rhythms of everyday life according to clock and calendar; they preached the control of passions and vices; and they emphasized the bourgeois ideal of the nuclear family as the basis of morality and prosperity.

The Catholic Church cautiously agreed with some elements of this program of reform. But while the Liberals diffused a republican national identity based on the war of 1856-57 and the sacrifice of Santamaría, the Church promoted the cult of the Virgin of los Ángeles. Colonial in origin and concentrated in Cartago, this belief acquired a national character after the 1880s. The Church preferred evangelizing to civilizing, and rejected Liberal attacks on its authority, especially over education and the family (civil marriage and divorce were approved in 1888).

The Church was supported by the majority of Costa Ricans, though the concern of that majority was more than simply religious. The Liberal program meant tighter administrative control, greater privatization of the land, persecution of alternative (and less expensive) medicine, and the outlawing of some popular customs considered to be "barbarous" (cockfighting, for example). On top of this, by making education mandatory, the Liberal reforms interfered with the labor contribution of children to the family economy. The resistance of the laboring classes to the Liberals never reached the point of open rebellion, but it came close.

Public school in Liberia, Guanacaste, 1909.

The Liberal reforms deepened a cultural divide, first visible in the 1840s, between comfortably-off urban sectors, with their cosmopolitan and secular politicians and intellectuals, and the mass of the population. A national identity centered on the National Campaign and the figure of Juan Santamaría was fundamental to overcoming this conflict. These symbols were systematically diffused by the press, the education system, and public monuments. The recovery of that experience, almost thirty years after its traumatic epilog, was done in a way that emphasized all that, according to the Liberals, distinguished Costa Ricans from the rest of Central Americans: their work ethic, their peaceful nature, their status as landowners and, above all, their membership in the white race.

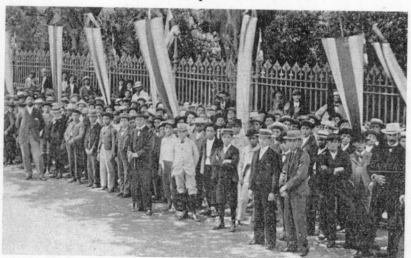

Independence Day, c. 1895.

The stress put on the racial identity of Costa Ricans could be excluding and discriminatory. This tendency, however, was counteracted by the education and the electoral systems, which were transformed into two fundamental avenues of social and cultural integration. The limits of discrimination are apparent in the fact that, despite being defined as a white society, Costa Rica adopted as a patron saint the black Virgin of los Angeles and a mulatto national hero in Juan Santamaría.

Procession of the Virgin of los Ángeles, c. 1926.

In this context boys and girls of different ethnic origin shared the same classrooms and, as electoral competition was consolidated, the parties opted to appeal to and mobilize whatever voters they could, regardless of the color of their skin. In fact, according to the electoral census of 1885, Guanacaste and Puntarenas, where indigenous and mulatto origins were more common, had a greater proportion of adults qualified to vote than the "white" provinces of San José and Cartago.

I, Santiago Córdova of Heredia, farmer... come before Your Excellency [Juan Rafael Mora] to humbly declare that the Eligibility Committee of my town has dealt me the notorious injury of not registering me on the list of eligible citizens... The only reason that the honorable Commission has given for refusing me the enjoyment of citizenship is its insistence that I do not own real property worth at least three hundred pesos, as required by the Newest Constitution [1848]... The Commission buries me... condemning me to live alone outside society and without that sweet name of citizen of the fatherland.

Santiago Córdova, 25 February 1859.

One of the factors that had contributed to the overthrow of Juan Rafael Mora was that during his presidency he failed to repeal the restrictions on voting rights enacted in the 1848 Constitution. After the coup d'etat of 1859 a new constitution was approved, and it practically established universal male suffrage for the first-round elections and reduced the requirements to be a second-round elector. These changes were consolidated in the 1871 Constitution that, though occasionally suspended, was in force until 1948. The marked extension of the right to vote stimulated a growing popular participation in politics over the course of the 1860s. This process, however, was interrupted by the authoritarian character of presidential succession between 1870 and 1885.

Elections for congressional deputies and city councilors continued, but the dictatorship of General Tomás Guardia and the government of General Próspero Fernández prevented competitive elections from becoming a

Barracks of Alajuela, 1909.

means to win the presidency. This began to change during the administration of Bernardo Soto. In the presidential elections of 1889, the Olympian clique tried to maintain itself in power through electoral fraud, after losing to the Church-backed candidate, José Joaquín Rodríguez. Spurred on by the clergy, peasants and artisans took up arms under the banner of the opposition, and surrounded the capital. A civil war was averted only when President Bernardo Soto agreed to a compromise that eventually allowed Rodríguez, the opposition candidate, to assume the presidency.

The popular uprising of 7 November 1889 is sometimes referred to as the origin of Costa Rican democracy. This is debatable, but the 1889 electoral

The call to arms was shouted throughout the neighboring towns... Within three hours... San José was surrounded by some 7,000 men, without counting those of Cartago, where 3,000 were concentrated, or those of Santo Domingo and Heredia, almost 2,000 of whom were making their way towards the latter city.

Account of the uprising of 7 November from the newspaper, *La Prensa Libre*, 13 November 1889.

campaign was the first in which two political parties competed to the bitter end and the opposition group rose up following victory at the polls. In the short term, José Joaquín Rodríguez and his successor and son-in-law, Rafael Iglesias inaugurated a new authoritarian interregnum (1890-1902). Still, during these years the opposition remained active and was able to compete with their own organizations in the elections that were periodically called, and thanks to which they gained important ground in the public sphere and in a political system that included the Congress and municipal government. The transition to an electoral democracy was under way.

The chamber of the old Costa Rican Congress, 1909.

CHAPTER 7

DIVERSIFICATION, CONFLICT AND DEMOCRACY (1890-1930)

The sale of coffee accounted for nearly 90 percent of the value of the country's exports between 1850 and 1890. This preeminence would be challenged by the banana industry, which was an indirect outgrowth of the coffee economy. Because of the impassable geography that separated the Central Valley from the Caribbean, almost all of Costa Rica's foreign trade went via the Pacific port. In 1870 the Guardia dictatorship attempted to resolve this contradiction with the European orientation of the country's economy and culture by contracting two large loans with English banking houses to build the Atlantic Railway.

The line went unfinished, however, due to technical difficulties, lack of funds and corruption (only one million

The railroad in the Central Valley, c. 1873.

It should come as no surprise that the people of Costa Rica, who have no pleasures beyond those that derive from the triumph of peace and the advantages of work and commerce, should perceive with such enthusiasm the first locomotive, pulled by oxen from the Pacific coast, make its entrance into the streets of Alajuela at an altitude of 4,200 feet above sea level. It arrived adorned with flags and accompanied by marching bands, like the conquistadors of bygone days, and it was followed by the multitudes and the preeminent residents of the city until it reached the railway station.

Account from the newspaper, *El Ferrocarril*, 6 April 1872.

of the 3.4 million pounds sterling borrowed actually found their way to the railway project). In 1884, the government of Próspero Fernández, short of options, signed a contract with Minor C. Keith in which the young US entrepreneur undertook to renegotiate the English debt and finish the railway. In exchange, a British financial concern in which Keith was a shareholder received a 99-year lease on the railway and the port facilities at Limón, and Keith himself was given ownership of vast extensions of the Caribbean lowlands (some 800,000 acres).

Keith's strategy was to finance part of the railway project by growing bananas and exporting them to the United States. The process culminated in Boston in 1899 with his role in founding the United Fruit Company. The Company quickly extended operations throughout the Caribbean basin and established a monopoly over the banana industry, making it the symbol of the economic face of US imperialism. The military and political dimensions of US power became apparent in 1898, when victory in the Spanish-American War left Washington with control over Puerto Rico and Cuba. United States hegemony in the region was cemented by its sponsorship of Panamanian independence from Colombia in 1903. The intervention gave the US exclusive rights over the inter-oceanic canal, which it finished building in 1914.

Costa Rica's national sovereignty had been successfully defended in 1856-57 but it was showing its limits by the turn of the century. The United Fruit Company controlled the country's Caribbean coast. To the south was the extraordinary US presence in Panama. To the north was Nicaragua, occupied by the Marines from 1912 to 1934. The weight of Washington in the economic and political life of Costa Rica grew increasingly decisive, the dependence intensifying dramatically after each world war (1914-18 and 1939-45).

In order to build the railroad, the various contractors imported thousands of foreign workers between 1870 and 1890. Most of them were Chinese, Italian and Afro-Caribbean

Loading bananas, 1909.

(largely Jamaican). Those who survived the unhealthy and dangerous working conditions and chose to stay on usually labored in the banana industry, in the Limón dockyards, and in small farming and petty commerce. The boom also attracted migrant workers from the Central Valley, Guanacaste and Nicaragua.

That much of the Caribbean coastal plain was an enclave run by a US-based company focussed the budding anti-imperialism of some Costa Rican politicians and intellectuals. This became mixed up with a racist anxiety about the anglophone and Protestant blacks who made up a majority of the population of Limón province. Meanwhile, especially after 1908, the expansion of banana cultivation was catastrophic for the Bribri natives of Talamanca and Sixaola. The banana zone was the most ethnically complex and politically sensitive region of Costa Rica.

The value of banana exports equalled that of coffee between 1910 and 1920, but the glory years of the industry were those stretching from 1890 to 1914: after the latter year the price paid for the fruit began to decline, rising slightly in the 1920s, only to plunge in 1927. United Fruit's predatory production process was itself largely responsible for this cycle of boom and bust. The profit margins of the company, which operated on an international scale, depended on the exploitation of virgin lands acquired for little

My mother told me that I were born twelve o'clock Sunday morning. My father was working for the United Fruit Company, and my mother used to bake. She did a lot of things. She was a midwife also, what you call a nurse... My father was a straw boss [a foreman]... It was in the banana plantations. My father leave Jamaica just like so many others... In those times you just up and down and nobody ask you any questions.

Joseph Spencer, resident of Cahuita, Limón, February 1976.

or no money. Once the lands were exhausted or invaded by disease, United Fruit simply abandoned them and began cultivation somewhere else. The Company adopted this tactic after 1930, when it moved its operations to the Pacific south region of Costa Rica (with devastating effects on the province of Limón), and the banana industry experienced another round of rapid growth.

The diversification of exports begun with bananas came to include other products of lesser importance whose take-off occurred after 1914. Sugar production, hitherto associated with peasant farming and the simple milling technique of the *trapiche*, now tended to concentrate itself in large capitalist ventures, with the cane processed

Sugar mill in Juan Viñas, Cartago, 1922.

in a more factory-like mill, or *ingenio*. Cacao production was controlled by United Fruit. Gold and silver was extracted from the mines of Montes del Aguacate and the Guanacastecan *cordillera* by foreign companies whose most conspicuous shareholder was none other than Minor C. Keith.

The export of hardwoods was important in Guanacaste. Logging meant the opening of new grazing land at the same time that the sale of wood provided capital to invest in better species of pasture grasses and new breeds of cattle. The growth of cattle ranching in Guanacaste was stimulated by the high price paid for cattle in the Central Valley, where coffee began to displace pastures after the 1840s. Between 1890 and 1930, the privatization of vast extensions of land converted the formerly

Corral at El Viejo, Guanacaste, 1909.

free-ranging people of the area, whose deep mulatto and indigenous roots combined with an earthy "cowboy" culture, into a poor peasantry with little land and few employment options.

In the valleys of the Reventazón and Turrialba, large agricultural estates raising cattle, growing sugarcane or cultivating coffee employed wage laborers who had little access to land. The social makeup of these peripheral areas was very different from that of the middle and the west of the Central Valley, where rural life was characterized by small and medium-sized family farms that were examples of a more successful peasant colonization of the land.

Starting in 1860, Costa Rica's coffee bourgeoisie had consolidated its control over credit with the creation of Central America's first banks. It now began to diversify its interests by investing in sugar, bananas, cacao, ranching, mining and light industry. Foreign capital, on top of participating in these ventures (and sometimes dominating them), controlled strategic services in the urban areas: electricity, telephones, and trams. In contrast, the state built a railroad to Puntarenas (1897-1910), which was electrified in the 1920s.

Gold mine in Abangares, Guanacaste, 1922.

Hand-in-hand with capitalist diversification came growing social conflict. On the Caribbean side, workers on the railway line conducted a number of wildcat strikes: the Chinese in 1874, the Jamaicans in 1879 and 1887, and

*The large landowners...,
in their limitless ambi-
tion to monopolize the
land, have no compas-
sion, not even for the in-
digent condition of our
families... Since the year
1908 we have witnessed
the destruction of large
villages that were built
up at great cost and with
great sacrifices.*

Peasants of Quebrada Grande
and Guardia, Guanacaste, June
1921.

the Italians in 1888. Banana workers struck in 1910, 1911, 1913, 1919 and 1921. Guanacaste was the scene of similar labor action in the mining areas of Abangares and Tilarán in 1906, 1907, 1911, 1919 and 1920. It was also the site of peasant protests against the privatization and concentration of land that peaked between 1920 and 1922.

The violence characteristic of labor conflict in the peripheral areas, which occasionally ended in death, was unusual in the Central Valley where the institutional channeling of conflict had been the norm since the late eighteenth century. However, the period from 1880 to 1930 was marked by a variety of struggles. The poor peasantry and the indigenous peoples made last ditch efforts to defend their communal lands. Small and middling coffee farmers organized to bring ever greater pressure to bear on the processors to purchase the crop at a better price. And in the urban areas artisans and workers organized and fought to have their salaries increased and their work day reduced.

The state cracked down on these popular challenges, but within limits. At the same time, the public power was not averse to intervening in the economic and social life of the country at critical moments, to regulate or arbitrate in labor disputes or to carry out small and localized land reforms. The attention that governments gave to the demands of the lower classes was not a product of accident or generosity of spirit. Following the twelve years of authoritarian government under José Joaquín Rodríguez (1890-94) and Rafael Iglesias (1894-1902), democracy made further gains. Thanks to the initiative of President Ricardo Jiménez, the direct vote was approved in 1913, and between 1925 and 1927 the secret vote was introduced. These reforms made political parties more responsive to voters.

The Society of Artisans of Costa Rica, c. 1924.

Democratic advances coexisted with electoral frauds and secret pacts. Fraud did not usually determine the results of elections: of the 16 presidential elections between 1890 and 1948, fraud only played a decisive role in four (1894, 1906, 1923 and 1948). At the same time, only one coup d'état occurred between 1902 and 1948. In 1917 Federico and Joaquín Tinoco deposed President Alfredo González Flores (1914-17), whose reformist government had established a state bank and introduced direct taxation. The Tinoco dictatorship was overthrown by a civil coalition in 1919. This victory accelerated the decline of the army and the expansion of police forces, a process that was reinforced by the poor performance of the Costa Rican military in the 1921 war with Panama sparked by a border dispute.

Cleto González Víquez on the campaign trail, c. 1927.

The gradual political integration of peasants, artisans and workers provided a solid base to the invention of the Costa Rican nation. Indeed the two processes reinforced one another. The popular classes were not only citizens in official speeches, but in political practice, and this was the basis of a strategic electoral connection between popular demands and public policies that was expressed in the national government's budget.

Expenditures on education, health, pensions, and public works (that also included education and public health infrastructure) rose from 24 percent of the government budget between 1890 and 1901, to 39 percent from 1920 to 1929. The same tendency was strengthened by the founding of two non-traditional political parties – the Reformist Party in 1923, whose leader was the charismatic populist, Jorge Volio; and the Communist Party in 1931, led by Manuel Mora. The Communists participated in elections during the 1930s and 1940s. Despite initially suffering some persecution, they won seats at the municipal and congressional level, and they consolidated strong constituencies among urban workers and laborers in the banana zones.

The civilizing mission of the Liberals had a paradoxical result. In 1930 a majority of Costa Rica's 500,000 people could read and write, accepted national values and symbols and participated in election campaigns. But the first three decades of the twentieth century were characterized by the erosion of the ideology of progress. The community of artists, writers, intellectuals and scientists that took shape between

The strength of the government, however, in reality rests far less upon the army than upon the disapproval of the people as a whole of any attempt to displace the constituted authorities in a disorderly manner, for the army itself is almost insignificant as a military force. There are a few troops in the barracks of the capital, but elsewhere order is maintained entirely by the civil police. It is a proud boast of the Costa Ricans that their government employs more school teachers than soldiers.

Dana Gardner Munro, 1918.

1860 and 1890 had devoted itself to legitimizing the "Republic of Coffee". A new intelligentsia emerged after 1900. Its leading lights were the poets Roberto Brenes Mesén and José María Zeledón (author of the lyrics to the national anthem), the novelist Joaquín García Monge, editor of the internationally respected *Repertorio Americano* from 1919 to 1958 (a periodical that contributed to disseminating the image of Costa Rica as a white republic in the outside world), and the writer and future Communist leader, Carmen Lyra. This more radical generation detected a sharp "social question" beyond the glitter of the golden bean: corrupt, greedy capitalists, and exploited and impoverished workers who had to be redeemed through an appropriate education.

Joaquín García Monge and his wife, Celia Carrillo, c. 1909.

The link between these young intellectuals and the artisans and workers of the urban world helped to radicalize working-class culture. During the period 1890-1930, the axis of industry was the shop more than the factory. Although these craftsmen worked for wages, their skill – as shoemakers, cabinetmakers, tailors, typesetters, bakers, masons – was essential to production, and they had a face-to-face relationship with their bosses. Anarchist and socialist ideas circulated through this distinct working-class culture, with its own clubs, associations, unions and newspapers. May Day was celebrated for the first time in 1913, and in February

1920 workers organized a co-ordinated
series of strikes in favor of the eight-
hour day, which was the culmination of
labor militancy during this era.

Large shoeshop, 1909.

The Church, the Liberal state, and
the young radical intelligentsia all
shared an obsession to evangelize, civilize and redeem the lower classes. The
source of this desire was a profound re-
jection of popular cultures whose irreverent style and plebeian concerns wor-
ried priests, good bourgeois citizens,
and progressive intellectuals alike. In
an effort to transform these cultures, a
network of state initiatives in social
control and social welfare took shape,

one that involved asylums, hospitals, prisons (including a modern penitentiary opened in 1909), and new ministries, like Public Health (created in 1927) and Labor (established in 1928). New institutions were created like the National Child Welfare Bureau (founded in 1930), and specific programs were undertaken, among them the campaigns against hookworm disease, begun in 1910 (aided by the Rockefeller Foundation starting in 1914), and the Drop of Milk, begun in 1913 to assist poor mothers in feeding their infants.

Far from being a *laissez-faire* state, starting at the end of the 19th century the Costa Rican state began to intervene systematically in society and culture, mostly via the education system. The emphasis given to health and hygiene reflected the Liberal concern with the high infant mortality rate of a country with a small population. This had led to the importing of manpower that was considered racially undesirable, particular that of Afro-Caribbeans. So, the origins of social policies that are among the most progressive in Latin America had a eugenic motivation that was closely linked to the insistence on a white racial national identity.

The efforts of politicians, ecclesiastics, and intellectuals to transform the behavior, the language and the world views of the plebs, particularly through education, were resisted and

Solón Núñez, promoter of the public health, 1910.

·

I accustom myself to bathing once a day. Why? The day that I do not bathe, even for good reason, is a day I spend feeling sad, ill-tempered and without desire to work.

Solón Núñez, *My Hygiene Catechism*, 1926.

manipulated by peasants, artisans and workers, who appropriated what they wanted to, discarding or adapting "decent" culture as they saw fit. Print culture provides an eloquent example. After 1880 the state published thousands of agricultural, scientific, historical and hygiene pamphlets for distribution among peasants and artisans. Readers in the lower classes availed themselves of this refined literature, while they simultaneously devoured the press of the period (notable for its yellow tendencies), entertained themselves with adventure or romance novels, and occasionally instructed themselves with writings of an anarchist or socialist bent.

The rise of mass culture further complicated the civilizing mission of those at the upper end of the social hierarchy. The theater had contributed to the kind of secularization of culture desired by the Liberals, but after 1914 it was displaced by the rapid expansion of the movies. By 1930 the country had experienced the successful debut and subsequent spread of radio.

Although occasionally surprising, the local contributions to mass culture were essentially limited. The principal products were football (soccer), which flourished in the working-class culture of the cities. While still largely amateur in nature the sport began to be transformed into mass entertainment during the 1920s. Popular music was

Movies? To suit every taste. Most of the films are from the United States, arranged in both English and Spanish, and the various theatres are always filled. The audience freely sympathizes with or disapproves of the scene before it. I remember that in "The Heart of Humanity" the villain was well hissed. The orchestra also comes in for notices from the audience.

US teacher Nina Weisinger, 1921.

The wedding went ahead [in 1937]; *I put the ring on my wife's finger and the mass ended... We left the church and headed for the Workers Center where we gathered with our family and friends for cake, coffee and lively dancing to the delightful tunes played by the Lubín Barahona Orchestra.*

Juan Rafael Morales, shoe-maker and union leader, 1993.

dominated by the *marimba* and the guitar in the cantinas, and by outdoor band concerts in the city plazas. This latter activity diversified after 1920, with the forming of groups and orchestras and the opening of dance halls and the country's first recording studios (a number of songs by Ricardo Mora became Latin American hits during the 1940s). The local newsreel appeared at least as early as 1910 when Amando Céspedes began to project his own version of "Pathé" in the country's first cinemas. And November 1930 saw the world-wide première of the first Costa Rican feature film, *El Retorno*, screened at the Variedades theater.

In the same way that they learned from mass culture to appreciate some of their own beliefs and behaviors, the increasingly literate and enfranchised popular sectors contributed to changes in national identity. They endorsed values that had been promoted by the turn-of-the-century generation of radical intellectuals: social justice, small agrarian property, and peace. Although peacefulness had been exalted as a particular Costa Rican virtue from earlier in the 19th century, the emphasis given to this characteristic in the 20th century gave it a new meaning. At the same time that it underlined the difference between Costa Ricans and the rest of Central Americans, it stressed the role played by the army of teachers against the army that had backed the Tinoco dictatorship and failed in the 1921 war with Panama.

Key to the success of this new message was the growing feminization of the teaching profession, especially primary school teachers. These women teachers played a central role in the Liberal program designed to civilize the popular sectors via the spread of values like discipline, patriotism, hard work, and hygiene. In this context women, whether organized in Catholic charity leagues or philanthropic organizations like the Drop of Milk, began to convert feminine qualities (maternity above all) into civic values – a process that gave birth to the invention in 1932 of Costa Rican Mother's Day. The decisive mobilization of women teachers against the Tinoco dictatorship in June 1919, which accelerated the fall of the regime, was proof of the new public roles that women were prepared to assume.

In the wake of this experience the Costa Rican Feminist League was founded in 1923 (though, curiously, among its leaders was Ángela Acuña, who had been an enthusiastic supporter of the Tinocos). The Feminist League mobilized successfully against unequal pay for women and men in the education system, but they could not get Congress to approve the vote for women in 1925. The League failed to win the franchise for women because, on the one hand, they were reluctant to

Maternity. Sculpture in stone. Francisco Zúñiga, 1935.

To help mothers with few resources, regardless of religion, to nourish their children from one day up to two years of age. No distinction will be made between married and unmarried mothers, since the primary goal of the society is to conserve children for the country.

Charter of the Drop of Milk Society, 1913.

summon working-class women to battle; on the other hand a reform of such
magnitude implied a huge degree of
electoral uncertainty and its approval
was too scary to the party leaderships
and their congressional representatives. Ironically, the democratic nature
of Costa Rican politics became an obstacle to the women's franchise.
Women won the right to vote only in
1949, in a rather undemocratic political context.

Many of the changes discussed
above also expressed the growth and
diversification of San José's urban

Women's Vote – the Day That They Get It. Newspaper cartoon. Paco Hernández, July 1923.

culture. Turn-of-the-century San José was dubbed a "metropolis in miniature" by one visitor from the United States. The description was not without foundation. The capital impressed foreigners with its national institutions (the Archive, the Library, the Museum, the Theater), its primary and secondary schools, its parks, alamedas and statues, its stores and bookshops, its Bohemian life, its growing number of newspapers and its diverse and active cultural milieu.

The center of San José witnessed impressive theatrical and dance performances (Ana Pavlova danced in the Teatro Nacional in 1917), and memorable interpretations of classical music: between 1894 and 1929 six symphony

San José is among the most enchanting of Central American cities. Its women are the most lovely of the five republics, and its society one of the most European and North American in style.

The great modernist Nicaraguan poet, Rubén Darío, 1891.

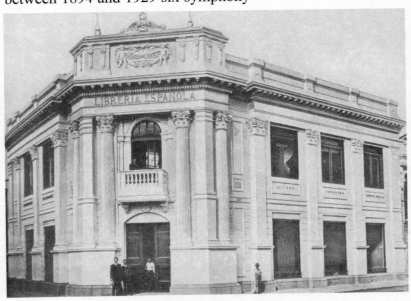

Librería Española bookstore, 1922.

orchestras were formed and the great Costa Rican tenor, Melico Salazar triumphed abroad. This was the pride of a Europeanized bourgeoisie and a stratum of scientists, artists and other intellectuals (some of them radical).

Public space, however, was disputed by a varied group of artisans and workers, and by a sub-culture of paupers, prostitutes and criminals (known during the era as "apaches"). The most plebeian and irreverent dimension of this urban popular culture was centered around the billiard hall and the

The Paperboy. Oil on canvas. Rigoberto Moya, 1929.

cantina. It expressed itself in a special slang, in aggressive drinking styles and in the use of drugs.

Opium and marijuana, whose use was not yet clearly illegal, had been consumed by a significant number of Costa Ricans since the end of the nineteenth century. The use of narcotics grew with the new century due to the expansion of medical prescriptions and pharmacies. Addiction to morphine was not unusual in certain upper crust circles, but in 1929 San José was shaken by a moral panic when it was discovered that hundreds of young artisans and workers were consuming heroin. Because of lax import-export controls, Costa Rica was also an important bridge in the international traffic in opium during the early decades of this century.

Two men dominated the presidency over the first four decades of this century: Cleto González Víquez (1906-10 and 1928-32) and Ricardo Jiménez (1910-14, 1924-28 and 1932-36). Despite the European charms of San José, the Costa Rica of "don Cleto" and "don Ricardo" was built on a fragile base. The economy remained dependent on the fortunes of one or two products, and growth was predicated on the parallel incorporation of more land and more labor, rather than on technological change. Social mobility was extremely limited and the abyss between the elites and the middle and

That's something that everyone knows [the identity of the heroin dealers] *and it's only us, those who don't have money to defend ourselves, it's only us who suffer persecution and arrest, while those who are trafficking are given every opportunity to defend themselves.*

A San José shoemaker and heroin user under police questioning, 1933.

lower classes tended to grow, something that would intensify after 1927. In that year, a drop in the price of Costa Rica's principal export products was the prelude to a terrible economic collapse.

Cleto González Víquez (1906) and Ricardo Jiménez Oreamuno (c. 1910), Costa Rica's "Olympian princes".

CHAPTER 8

THE DEPRESSION, SOCIAL REFORM AND CIVIL WAR (1930-1950)

Costa Rica's Liberal republic was built on the belief that given free rein a capitalist economy based on agricultural exports would lead to civilization and prosperity for all. That certainty evaporated with the New York stock market crash of 1929 and the subsequent global economic collapse. In discrediting free-market dogma, the great slump paved the way for the triumph of a new philosophy based on growing state intervention.

The Costa Rican economic collapse was sharp indeed. Between 1929 and 1932, the value of exports fell from 18 to 8 million dollars, and that of imports dropped from 20 to 5 million. The crisis of the export sector also led to a drastic decrease in the customs revenues that were vital to

Workers pick coffee near San José, 1922.

I arrived at the finca called «El Bosque» [The Jungle] and I found that the workers were still unhappy about the miserable salaries and the awful way they had to earn them; and that they had sent a petition to the Manager of the Company, and another to the President of the Republic, outlining their hardships and the dangerous lives they led; neither of the two... had sent them a single word in reply and so I told them that the only road left was to begin a˙general strike.

Banana worker and Communist organizer, Carlos Luis Fallas Sibaja, October 1934.

state finances, resulting in an acute deficit from 1929 to 1936. Farming families were sheltered from the worst effects of the Depression, but all salaried workers were hit hard.

The strongest popular reaction against this situation came from the young Communist Party's most loyal constituencies: urban workers, and laborers in the banana zone. The 1933 march of the unemployed in San José ended in a violent confrontation with police, and in August-September of 1934 thousands of banana workers went on strike under Communist leadership, paralyzing United Fruit operations on the Caribbean coast.

To deal with the crisis, government began to intervene more actively in the economy. In 1933 the Institute for the Defense of Coffee was created to regulate relations between farmers and processors. In 1935 a minimum wage was legislated for agricultural workers, and in 1936 bank reforms were undertaken to give the state more control over the money supply. Suspension of payments on the foreign debt in 1932 freed resources to pay for the import of essential goods, and to increase government spending. The financing of public works, designed to reduce unemployment, more than tripled between 1932 and 1939, and practically defined the presidency of León Cortés (1936-40), dubbed the government of "cement and iron".

Despite the hardships that it imposed on many, the Depression fomented a modest expansion in import-substitution industry. It was also a fertile era for Costa Rican culture. Between 1928 and 1937 annual plastic arts exhibitions promoted the rise of a movement in sculpture that sought inspiration in the indigenous past, and whose leading exponents were Juan Manuel Sánchez and Francisco Zúñiga. A school of landscape painting also formed during this era, concentrating on rural scenes of the Central Valley, and with a particular fixation on the adobe house. During the 1940s, the novel of social conscience reached its peak in works that dwelled on strategies of survival and forms of struggle

Adobe House. Oil on canvas. Fausto Pacheco, no date.

among workers and peasants. The most famous of these is *Mamita Yunai* (1941) by Carlos Luis Fallas, which portrays life in the Caribbean empire of the United Fruit Company.

The Communist Party celebrates the publication of *Mamita Yunai*, July 1941.

The economy showed signs of recovery in 1936, as coffee prices stabilized and banana operations expanded on the Pacific south. In 1939, however, the outbreak of World War II put an end to the recovery. The closing of European markets, formerly the destination of 50 percent of Costa Rica's exports, meant a redirection of trade to the United States. Unfortunately the US bought coffee at an inferior price and could not absorb all the shipments of bananas.

Despite declining state revenues, an ambitious program of social reform was undertaken by the government of Rafael Ángel Calderón Guardia (1940-44). The University of Costa Rica was created (1940), a Social Security system was established (1941), Social Guarantees were written into the Constitution and a Labor Code was enacted (1943). Although its real effects were limited, this transformation laid the foundations of the welfare state, while at the same time intensifying political instability.

The social reform's origins certainly lie in the interventionist tradition of the Costa Rican state that can be traced back to the end of the 19th century. It also responded to the prior struggles of workers to improve their working and living conditions. But the reform process also had an important electoral dimension. Given that Costa Rica was one of the few countries in the world where democracy had not collapsed during the 1930s, the Communist Party remained legal (again, an exception in Central America) and was able to have success at the ballot box during this era. Thanks to its union organizations and the presence it enjoyed in the public sphere with its newspaper, *Trabajo*, the Communists based their vote-getting strategy on a systematic denunciation of social problems that had worsened in the crisis of the 1930s.

In the face of the growing Communist threat a Catholic wing began to form in the National Republican Party (founded in 1931 and made into the country's leading political organization over the next ten years). Like the

The reforms being passed have no objective, no relevance, and no opportunity [of succeeding]. *They mean nothing to the people... who are calling to the high heavens... for bread, clothes, welfare... freedom. The reforms... have a hollow ring. They are pure poetic claptrap, campaign literature, and – above all – lies.*

Three-time former President Ricardo Jiménez Oreamuno, May 1942.

"Buy *Trabajo*" (the Communist weekly), October 1938.

Communists, this faction called for institutional reforms to confront the social question, but with the fundamental goal to undermine the electoral strategy of their foes on the left. The anti-Communism intensified by the outbreak of the Spanish Civil War in 1936 strengthened this group, whose leader was Calderón Guardia.

The Calderonistas' anxiety about confronting the Communists was shared by the Catholic Church hierarchy, and especially the then Bishop of Alajuela, Víctor Manuel Sanabria. The ecclesiastics, though, also pushed their own agenda of overturning the anticlerical legislation passed by the Liberals at the end of the 19th century. During the first decades of the 20th

The celebration of the 300th anniversary of the Virgin of los Ángeles was dominated by anti-Communism. The placard announces: *Sovereign Queen do not allow Russia to impose its communist doctrine on Costa Rica so that she always may confess to Christ the redeemer*, 1935.

century Catholic deputies (including some priests) had tried to repeal these laws in Congress, but without success.

Preparing for the 1940 presidential elections, the Calderonistas secured two basic accords. The first was with the followers of the incumbent President, León Cortés. It guaranteed Cortesista support for Calderón Guardia's presidential bid in return for subsequent Calderonista support for Cortés to get a second term as president in 1944. The second deal was with Sanabria, on the verge of becoming Archbishop of Costa Rica. It delivered the prelate's support for the coming (and still largely under wraps) Calderonista program of social reform in return for their commitment to overturn anticlerical legislation.

The social reform, then, was at the outset a product of electoral calculation: in carrying out a series of measures to answer demands from the popular sectors, the Calderonistas expected to take votes away from a Communist Party that had become the principal adversary of the National Republican Party in the cities. By stealing the more moderate parts of the Communist reform program, the Communist Party would have to radicalize its demands. This would move it away from the centrist position it had adopted after 1935 (in line with the changes in the international communist strategy of the day), a more moderate stance that

[W]e never imagined that legislation like that could exist in that time... Calderón's proposal caught us with our guard down and we were obliged to support it in order to conserve our influence.

Luis Carballo, Communist Party leader, 1969.

was in good measure behind the party's success at the polls.

This strategy gave Calderón Guardia a huge victory in 1940 with over 80 percent of the vote. But his government soon found itself facing a growing opposition that had a variety of sources. Some sectors of the merchant elite were hostile to the progressive elements of the reforms. Furthermore, Costa Rica's declaration of war against Nazi Germany (at the behest of the US) hurt the coffee elite of German origin, who had their properties expropriated and had to languish in detention centers. Inflation badly damaged the fleeting prosperity of the middle class. The political tension was aggravated by a patronage machine that favored Calderón

Manuel Mora, Monseñor Sanabria and Calderón Guardia, 1943.

Guardia's family and friends over other allies whose support had been crucial for his landslide victory.

Calderón Guardia's actions led to increasing confrontation with the Cortesistas, and it culminated in 1941 when the faction around Cortés opted to abandon the National Republican Party and began a systematic smear campaign against the government. The split of a party that had won the 1940 presidential election with a huge majority opened up an opportunity for the Communists. They began to get closer to the government with the goal of participating in a social reform that, originally, had been designed against them and that seriously threatened to make their demands obsolete. The first overtures were made in 1941, and the pact was cemented in 1943. The alliance received the blessing of Sanabria, by then the reformist Archbishop of San José. Church leaders had reason to be pleased with Calderón Guardia: in 1940 religious instruction had been reintroduced into the schools and in 1942 the ban on establishing religious orders in the country was lifted. Despite this, Sanabria's support for the alliance profoundly split the clergy.

This political marriage was denounced by the opposition as "Calderocomunismo", but its legitimacy was strengthened by the unusual circumstances of the alliance between the United States and the Soviet Union in

Another long discussion dealt with the attitude of the Church toward the Communist group... After a long and heated discussion in this regard, one Juan Rafael Calzada... stated that he had been told by Monseñor Solís, the Bishop of Alajuela, that Solís is organizing a group of anti-Communist Priests whose purpose will be to combat the growth of Communism through the Church.

Report on a group of young capitalists organized to combat Communism. US Embassy in San José, August 1944.

The Archbishop [Sanabria] *described Manuel Mora as both an intelligent and sincere man and said that of all the politicians he knew he thought Manuel Mora the most sincere in his desire to help the poor. He added that there is no doubt that Mora and his followers are in sympathy with Russia, but said that he did not know whether or not there was actual contact between Russia and the Vanguardia Popular* [Communist Party]. *He pointed out in this connection that when Mora made a visit to Mexico recently, he had not called on the Soviet Ambassador.*

US Ambassador in San José, Hallett Johnson, April 1945.

the war against fascism that culminated in 1945 with the defeat of Germany and Japan. The Cold War between the US and the USSR that followed World War II, however, made the alliance between Calderón Guardia and Manuel Mora's Communist Party increasingly difficult to justify, given Costa Rica's location in what US politicians liked to call their "back yard".

Nevertheless, the polarization of Costa Rican politics had preceded the Cold War. The victory of Teodoro Picado, the incumbent party's candidate in the elections of 1944, was declared fraudulent by the anti-Calderón Guardia opposition, deepening the crisis. The deterioration of the political system's credibility was linked to a change in the geographical patterns of electoral fraud.

Prior to 1944 the majority of accusations of fraud came from the provinces of Guanacaste, Puntarenas and Limón. After 1944, by contrast, the majority came from the Central Valley, a change that is explained by the fact that this part of the country, where about 74 percent of the electorate lived, was the stronghold of the opposition. And so this was where the political fight intensified. Given Picado's huge margin of victory, however, it is clear that even had all the accusations of fraud been proven he still would have won the election without those votes.

The impact of these changing patterns of fraud was magnified by the media that backed the opposition. The growing indignation over what had happened had a lot to do with the fact that fraudulent practices were now affecting a population that was not made up predominately of poor peasants or banana workers, and was not of indigenous or mulatto origin, but one whose ballast was made up of small and medium farmers and merchants who considered themselves to be "white" Costa Rican citizens. The political culture of the coastal provinces, with its greater degree of abuse and coercion, proved intolerable in the more urbanized and literate Central Valley.

The economic recovery after 1945 was unable to mollify growing mistrust in the political system, and the

Opposition march of women calling for electoral guarantees, August 1947.

This is a report of the Strike Committee [of businessmen who had organized a shutdown] *to the Costa Rican citizenry. The Strike remains in effect throughout the territory of the Republic... Only a very few businesses owned by Calderonistas remain open, and they are being placed on a list of enemies of the national cause.*

Bulletin from the «Huelga de Brazos Caídos», July 1947.

explosion of terrorist bombs in the cities became a frequent event. Picado's administration (1944-48) brought the social reforms to an end, split with the Communists and attempted to provide the opposition with guarantees in the new electoral code of 1946. But it was to no avail. The tendency was reinforced by the sudden death of León Cortés in March 1946. Despite his attacks on the government, Cortés was looking for a negotiated way out of the conflict. His death strengthened hardline sectors of the opposition who nominated Otilio Ulate, the editor of the *Diario de Costa Rica*, as their presidential candidate to challenge Calderón Guardia's second bid for the presidency.

The election campaign of 1948 was waged amid extreme polarization and its results were surprising: in the presidential elections Ulate beat Calderón Guardia by 10,943 votes, but in

Otilio Ulate campaigning in San Ignacio de Acosta, San José province, January 1948.

the election of congressional deputies Calderonistas and Communists defeated the opposition by 12,308 votes. As if this was not enough, thousands of Calderonista and Communist voters alleged that they had been denied the vote through inappropriate management of the Electoral Registry, a body whose director was closely identified with the hard-line sectors of the opposition. In these circumstances the Congress, dominated by Calderón Guardia supporters, annulled the results of the presidential elections on the first of March. Eleven days later, without waiting for the conclusion of negotiations between Calderón Guardia and Ulate to find a peaceful solution, a renegade member of the elite called José Figueres rose up in arms. The Civil War had begun.

The two forces that would emerge victorious from the armed conflict of 1948 had been on the margins of political life prior to that year. The Center for the Study of National Problems was founded in 1940 by young intellectuals and professionals. The Center's leading figures were the lawyer, Rodrigo Facio and the historian, Carlos Monge. Its members resented the stranglehold that the coffee oligarchy and United Fruit had on the economy. At the same time they were virulently anti-Communist. Their sympathy for social reform was linked to a fierce critique of the government, which

One of the dominant attitudes of the Centro has been its consistent and bitter opposition to Communism... the Centro [Center for the Study of National Problems] *has as assets youth, intelligence, financial resources, and the only concrete program for Costa Rica save that of the Vanguardia Popular Party. Its future will be largely what it chooses to make.*

Report from the US Embassy in San José, October 1943.

Carlos Monge Alfaro in 1972, when he declared: *More than simply possible, it is necessary to implant a socialist-style regime in Costa Rica.*

they accused of being corrupt, antiquated, unjust and incompetent.

The agricultural entrepreneur, José Figueres Ferrer had spent two years in Mexican exile (1942-44) after a volatile radio speech attacking Calderón Guardia. Upon returning, he continued his criticisms of the government and formed the Democratic Action Party. In 1945 this party merged with the Center for the Study of National Problems to create the Social Democratic Party which threw its support behind León Cortés and then, after the unexpected death of Cortés, behind Ulate.

The formation of a rebel army, however, long preceded the elections of 1948. During his exile in Mexico, Figueres made contact with the Caribbean

Legion, an organization of exiles whose goal was to overthrow the dictators of the region. The return to Costa Rica in 1944 gave Figueres the opportunity to start figuring in the national political scene and to start training irregular troops at his ranch in San Isidro de El General.

On 16 December 1947, almost two months prior to the elections, Figueres signed the "Pacto del Caribe", in which he agreed that, once he was in power, Costa Rica would serve as a base for overthrowing the rest of the tyrants of the region. The accord was sponsored by Juan José Arévalo, the President of Guatemala, and it was from Guatemala, on 13 March 1948, that a plane arrived in San Isidro with men and weapons for the rebel army.

The military option was the only one that might permit Figueres and his supporters to take power since their electoral support was insignificant. This explains the intransigent stance they took during the post-electoral negotiations. The annulment of the presidential elections gave them the excuse they needed to act before any possible compromise could be reached between Ulate and Calderón Guardia, and to begin a war in the name of the defense of democratic suffrage, which in reality was fought for something much more than the vote. (In fact, recent research strongly suggests that Calderón Guardia actually won in 1948).

On February 19th the [National Electoral] tribunal had only scrutinized the votes of the two smallest provinces of the country (Limon and Puntarenas), and the results seemed to bear out the claim of the government parties, that thousands of voters were unable... to go to the polls. That this should have happened in two provinces in which the electorate would undoubtedly have given the Government parties a large majority – a fact which is admitted by the opposition – seems to lend strength and reason to the claims of the vanquished parties.

F. G. Coultas, British Minister in San José, February 1948.

The corpses had been splashed with gasoline and they burned like torches, curling up as they were consumed by the flames, offering up scenes worthy of Dante. I could appreciate the fear reflected in the pale faces of children and women, who carried large sacks with their belongings in a desperate attempt to rescue what was most necessary and indispensable.

Testimony of a combatant, March 1948.

The Tragedy of Costa Rica, memoirs of a Calderonista exile, 1951.

The armed conflict lasted five weeks, from 12 March to 19 April, 1948. More than 4,000 people died, making this by far the worst outbreak of political violence in Costa Rican history. Figueres' "Army of National Liberation" quickly defeated and dispersed the rinky-dink Costa Rican army, and prepared to face off against the pro-government militias holding San José (the famous "mariachis"). The foreign diplomatic corps negotiated a ceasefire and a political pact to end the war: Calderonistas surrendered in return for a promise that their property and lives would be respected, and the Communists did so provided that the social reforms would be kept intact and their Party would not be suppressed.

Figueres quickly broke key parts of the agreement by outlawing the Communist Party, purging the public sector of Calderón Guardia supporters, and sending thousands into exile. The victorious leader also failed to fulfill the Pacto del Caribe, refusing to allow Costa Rica to be used as a base to launch attacks against neighboring dictators. Neither did he hand over power to Ulate, instead signing an agreement with him on 1 May 1948 that gave Figueres power as the head of a transitional Junta that would last eighteen months.

The most famous decree of the Junta was to abolish the army, an act that had great symbolic importance and closed off avenues for future militarization. The Junta also agreed on an extraordinary tax of 10 percent on all capital over 50,000 colones (about US $8,000) and nationalized the banks, thus eliminating the control of the coffee bourgeoisie over credit, which was seen as an essential part of a strategy of promoting economic diversification. The social reforms were strengthened, the Costa Rican Electricity Institute (ICE) was established, and a greater rate of taxation was imposed on United Fruit exports.

A constituent assembly was inaugurated on 15 January 1949 to write a new constitution for the so-called Second Republic. Dominated by supporters of Ulate, it rejected the constitution

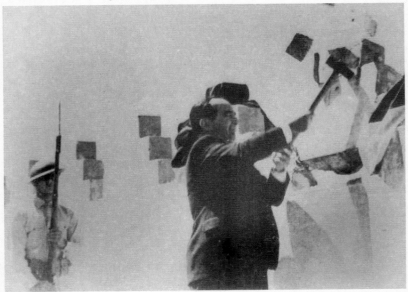

Figueres during the act that abolished the army, 1948.

Does anybody fail to see that this costly and ruinous comedy [of electoral politics], *despite its democratic appearance, is nothing but camouflage for a selfish oligarchy that has dominated Costa Rica for some time?... Peasants have their votes bought or extorted from them by the big landowner, who is the boss of their town; he in turn sells it in exchange for something, an appointment or a promise of influence, to the city boss; and the city boss deals it in turn, for a congressional seat or a ministerial chair, to the San José politicians, themselves the bosses of the Republic... Everything else is a lie – liberty a lie, democracy a lie...*

Mario Sancho, 1935.

prepared by the Junta, and ended up reinventing the old Liberal charter of 1871. The few additions, however, were extremely significant. The power of the Executive was weakened, and the right of women to vote was enshrined, as was that of the Afro-Caribbean population. The office of the Auditor General was established, along with a code regulating the Civil Service and a charter for autonomous institutions. Finally, the Supreme Electoral Tribunal was created, which little by little brought under control fraudulent practices in national elections.

This vast program of institutional change was ideologically justified as necessary to found the Second Republic (a century after the first had been declared). The origins of such a grandiose idea were related to a polemical pamphlet written in 1935 by Mario Sancho, *Costa Rica: The Switzerland of Central America*. Sancho emphasized the weaknesses and vices of Costa Rican society, even as he left out mention of its strengths and virtues. His totalizing critique was appropriated by the young renegades of the Center for the Study of National Problems to justify the complete transformation of Costa Rica that they saw as necessary to overcome the corruption and decadence that they felt predominated in the country.

This transformation, according to Rodrigo Facio, would have to be done using technical criteria rather than by pandering to patronage and political interests. The most apt for performing this task were the young professionals and intellectuals of the Center and their allies, the Figuerista entrepreneurs. To implement the project they would first need to gain political power, which they achieved following the Civil War of 1948, and then they would have to consolidate an electoral constituency, something that would require dismantling two of the principal political powers of the day: Calderonismo and Communism. Clearing the electoral arena so that a new party could grow was precisely what the Figueristas did. Once the mandate of the Junta was up, Figueres permitted Ulate to assume the presidency, and set out with his closest

It's true that some revolutionary leaders, drunk with gunpowder and victory, at first would have liked to ignore the election of February 8 [1948], but later those leaders reflected on things in more sober fashion and realized what the popular feeling was and changed their attitude.

Rodrigo Facio, 1949.

Rector of the University of Costa Rica, Rodrigo Facio, lunches with faculty and students in the 1950s.

I swear that one day, be it tomorrow, be it months from now, when the sun rises over the fatherland, it will light up, to the rejoicing of our nation and of all other nations, the grandiose spectacle of the Second Republic of Costa Rica.

José Figueres Ferrer, May 1944.

allies to organize the Partido Liberación Nacional (the Party of National Liberation), founded in 1951.

In the other countries of Central America, the crisis of 1930 was characterized by the rise of military dictatorships: Ubico in Guatemala (1931-44), Hernández Martínez in El Salvador (1931-44), Carías in Honduras (1933-48) and Somoza in Nicaragua (1936-79). A wave of democratization swept the isthmus between 1944 and 1954, but it dissipated as the polarization of the Cold War breathed new life into another crop of tropical tyrannies supported by the United States. In this context, Costa Rica's political project was exceptional indeed: social justice and state modernization would be converted into the basis of political democracy.

Figueres in the Victory Parade, 1948.

CHAPTER 9

THE GOLDEN AGE OF
THE MIDDLE CLASS
(1950-1978)

By 1978 Costa Rica could boast social indicators far better than those of most Third World countries, despite a demographic explosion that increased the population from some 800,000 to almost 2 million between 1950 and 1973. The average Costa Rican could expect to live to the age of 70, infant mortality was a healthy 20 per thousand live births, and 90 percent of the people over 10 years old were literate. Three-quarters of the labor force were covered by Social Security, and unemployment hovered at a mere 5 percent.

This social improvement rested on a spectacular wave of growth, itself the product of the awesome expansion of the global economy after World War II. Between 1944 and 1952, banana exports rose from 3.5 million to

First day of classes at the University of Costa Rica, March 1971.

18 million crates annually, and the price of coffee rose from 9 to 68 dollars per quintal between 1940 and 1956. The traditional export sector generated extraordinary profits that were channeled through the state banking system to provide financing for technological improvements and agricultural and industrial diversification.

Coffee plantations tripled their productivity between 1950 and 1970, thanks to the use of agro-chemicals, a practice that was also intensified in the banana industry to further enhance cultivation of disease-resistant varieties of the fruit. Competition was another stimulus to innovation. The state authorized operations by three new foreign banana companies between 1956 and 1965, and facilitated the rise of local banana entrepreneurs who produced an increasing amount of the fruit under contract with the multinationals. In the face of this challenge, the United Fruit Company got into stock-raising, the cultivation of African palm and the manufacture of oil, lard and margarine for the local market.

The income distribution policies of Liberación Nacional increased the spending power of the populace. Greater numbers of consumers provided a basis for the capitalization of other activities, particularly rice and dairy farming. Local consumption also helped somewhat in the take-off in the sugar and beef sectors after 1960. The

A plan was initiated to provide credit for coffee and cacao, in the hopes of improving our position in terms of foreign currency reserves by increasing the productivity of our export goods; in 1954 more than four million colones were devoted to the plan, involving not only financing but also technical help from specialized agencies of the Ministry of Agriculture and Industry.

Jorge Rossi, Minister of Finance, May 1955.

key to the success of these industries, though (besides access to bank credit), was the US decision to eliminate the Cuban sugar quota following the revolution of 1959, and the rise of fast foods in the United States.

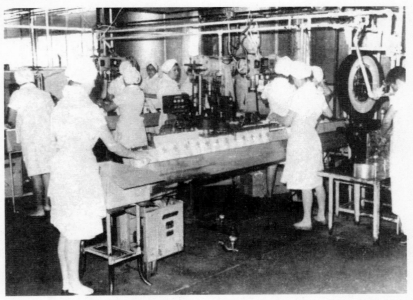

Processing lard at the Numar plant (then a subsidiary of the United Fruit Company), c. 1960s.

During the 1950s, the main efforts at diversifying the economy took place in the agricultural sector. The real take-off in industry occurred in 1963 when Costa Rica joined the Central American Common Market. For a decade, industrial growth was vertiginous: over 100 companies were formed in Costa Rica between 1963 and 1975, the majority of them foreign-owned. The weight of tobacco, beverages and food-processing in the make-up of local industry became proportionally smaller as a chemical and metal-mechanical sector expanded. In the process, the workshops of days gone by gave way to the impetuous advance of the factory.

Workers at the Costa Rican Tobacco Company, c. 1950s.

A new public sector nurtured and guided this economic growth, and itself grew and diversified at an incredible rate. The number of state employees increased ninefold between 1948 and 1979, when 130,000 public sector workers made up 18 percent of the labor force. In line with a tendency towards a decentralization of power, 75 new autonomous public agencies were created during the same period.

Public investment manifested itself in schools, high schools, roads, highways, hydroelectric plants, health clinics, hospitals and other infrastructure projects. Neither was the formation of "human capital" (that is, people) forgotten. The direction of public administration was assumed by an expanding group of technicians and professionals, graduates of the University of Costa Rica and foreign centers of higher learning.

Insisting on technical rather than political criteria for the development of the public sector had been a central thread in the discourse of Roberto Brenes Mesén, and later was a core part of the program espoused by the Center for the Study of National Problems, based to a great extent on the thinking of Rodrigo Facio. Ironically, the putting into

Such intervention [by the state must be]... *undertaken by autonomous Institutions, that is to say, not by the ministries directly, where politics gets in the way, but rather by technical functionaries, independent of the vicissitudes of politics, who are specialists in the field.*

Rodrigo Facio, 1949.

Figueres and Monseñor Odio at the official opening of the Tibás electric plant, San José province, 1956.

One would have to say that the autonomous institutions have served Liberación Nacional, because the party has staffed those institutions with its own supporters and maintained in this way a share of political power even during the periods in which the party has been in opposition.

Ex-President Mario Echandi, 1975.

practice of this "social engineering" credo, which was supposed to depoliticize the exercise of power, converted public employees into faithful followers of Liberación Nacional. The party used this technocratic thrust to disguise traditional forms of electoral patronage, and to propagate a statist ideology.

In the perspective of Liberación, state financing (using the revenues provided by coffee and bananas) was the key to opening new frontiers of capital accumulation outside the control of the traditional bourgeoisie. The public sector had to put its bank resources, its specialists and its infrastructure at the disposal of private capital, in particular that of small and medium-sized business.

José Figueres transfers power to Daniel Oduber, 8 May 1974.

The Liberacionista Utopia was a world of cheap credit, endless salary increases, support for co-operatives (the most successful of which were those of coffee growers, who founded 23 between 1963 and 1972), stable public employment, opportunities for social mobility through the expansion of secondary and university education, and the strengthening of the internal market. The partial realization of this dream meant a significant improvement in people's living conditions. The main beneficiaries of the boom were the urban and rural middle classes, who prospered with the growth of export activities, the expansion of the public sector, the increase in the size of cities and the expansion of industry. The rise of strong unions of public employees that occurred in the 1960s gave ballast to middle-class prosperity.

Economic expansion combined with social justice provided legitimacy to democratic politics over the long term, but the short-term consolidation of democracy proved difficult. The end of the Civil War did not bring a quick return to stability. In December 1948 Calderón Guardia let loose an invasion from Nicaragua that was neutralized by the intervention of the Organization of American States (OAS). In April 1949 the Minister of Public Security in the interim Junta, Édgar Cardona, staged an unsuccessful coup d'etat whose objective was to roll back the

A number of social experiences, especially in Costa Rica, show that the existence of strong nucleuses of small landowners are a moderating element in economic and social development..., a force for political and social equilibrium... and the strengthening of democratic institutions... Exotic and totalitarian ideologies have never succeeded in penetrating where small landowners have economic and political strength...

Future president Luis Alberto Monge, 1961.

In order to reveal the communist affiliation of Mr. Figueres, I will soon provide to the appropriate authorized international organization proof of the identity and the ideas that Mr. Figueres shares with Marxist philosophy, including an unpublished article written by a North American journalist who visited my country at the end of 1953, and to whom Figueres declared that a Soviet invasion of Alaska would be very healthy because it would galvanize the Americas.

Ex-President Otilio Ulate, 1954.

bank nationalization and the 10 percent tax on all capital over 50,000 colones.

The ascent of Ulate to the presidency in November 1949 was the beginning of a period of fragile stability that disappeared following Figueres' 1953 victory at the polls. The first Liberación Nacional government quickly ran into serious efforts to destabilize it, promoted by opposition sectors allied with key players in the US government who considered Figueres a Communist. The process culminated in 1955 when Costa Rica was invaded once again from Nicaragua, though this effort also failed following the intervention of the OAS.

The abolition of the armed forces undoubtedly had a good deal to do with the failures of these attempts to destabilize the Figueres government. The efforts themselves, however, led to divisions within the ranks of Liberación Nacional, and the party split before the 1958 elections, costing them the presidency. The opposition that year nominated the exiled Calderón Guardia to be a congressional candidate for San José, and had as a presidential candidate Mario Echandi who, according to one of the leaders of the 1955 invasion, had actively collaborated with the attempt to overthrow the government that year.

The initial impulse of some of the important Liberación Nacional leaders, including Figueres himself, was to refuse to recognize the Echandi victory.

In the end, however, that move was rejected and this contributed decisively to consolidating electoral democracy in Costa Rica. Echandi's government (1958-62) contributed to this process, too, by promoting a general amnesty that allowed Calderón Guardia to return to Costa Rica and assume the deputy's seat he had won.

In spite of the 1958 defeat, Liberación Nacional did not lose its ideological and political leadership. The party also had a great advantage in that the opposition that took shape after 1950 was largely a fragile and incoherent coalition of all those who had lost out in 1948, essentially made up of the traditional coffee elite, the followers of

Calderón Guardia and his son, Rafael Ángel Calderón Fournier, return to Costa Rica, 1958.

You have quite a few investments in the [Latin] American dictatorships. The aluminum companies take out bauxite almost free of charge. Your... state functionaries and... magnates are treated like royalty... Certain businessmen bribe the ruling dynasties with their millions for the right to hunt on the grounds of their estates. The money is an income tax deduction... Meanwhile, our women are abused and our men are castrated in torture chambers, and our illustrious professors disappear with gloomy regularity... When one of your legislators calls all this «collaboration in the war on communism», 180 million Latin Americans are overwhelmed with the urge to spit.

José Figueres before the Committee on Foreign Relations of the United States Congress, June 1958.

Ulate, those of Calderón Guardia, and the Communists (formerly the bitterest of enemies). Victory by the opposition in the elections of 1958 and 1978 was only possible because Liberación defeated itself through internal divisions; in 1966, a strong campaign accusing its candidate, Daniel Oduber, of being a communist was decisive in defeating Liberación.

The deep conservatism of the opposition became more exaggerated in the context of the Cold War. This made it easier for Liberación to assume the role of a progressive party. Aside from promoting modernization, Liberación governments practiced a more active international diplomacy in defense of the prices of export products, and critical of the United States' support for the dictatorships of the region. This did not stop Costa Rica from supporting the blockade of Cuba and generally acting as a faithful ally of Washington's crusade against communism.

This "golden age" of growth with income redistribution was not without its losers: the peasantry, wage laborers and the environment. Small farmers of grain and other basic foodstuffs, although they often tried to form co-operatives and adopt more modern techniques like the use of agro-chemicals, were displaced by large-scale capitalist agriculture. They were condemned to a future of frustration, poverty, expropriation, exodus and squatting. The rise of agri-business accentuated the concentration of land in fewer hands, and subjected the environment to an unprecedented assault. Deforestation was particularly acute in the banana sector, and it also accompanied the growth of extensive cattle ranching in Guanacaste. The massive expansion in the use of agro-chemicals left behind contaminants that remained invisible between 1950 and 1970, and whose full effects are only now becoming apparent.

Juan Rafael Morales, 1999.

The persecution of Calderonistas and Communists which began in 1948 lingered on in the years that followed. Although the left maintained its influence among banana workers (the most combative sector of labor from 1950 to 1970), the organizations and the culture of the urban working class tended to disappear. The identity and powerbase that they had built after 1890 fell victim to the anti-union offensive of the state and of employers, to urban growth and to a new kind of industrialization. Manual skills which had been essential in the workshop were no longer necessary on the factory assembly line. Industrial growth after 1963 was based on a working class whose members had no links to the labor traditions dating from the turn of the century.

The Communists, confronted by the outlawing of their party and a loss of influence among the new working

Avanti was the first real factory. Okay, this is where the methods of production changed... At that point the shoemaker stops being a shoemaker, and becomes a shoe worker who puts in eyelets or tongues, or who just does insoles or operates one machine... He's no longer an artisan, he's a piece of machinery, who's not allowed to speak, and who has to be connected to the machine, to the switch.

Juan Rafael Morales, shoemaker, 1987.

I was a person who always had an interest in involving housewives as participants and leaders because ever since I've had a sense of being involved in the struggle I've believed in the solidity of women when they are involved. Women are the ones who most feel the need to stand up for a movement, be it against the increase in electricity rates, or water rates, or the rising cost of bread, or transportation... Maybe it's tough getting them out, but there's no doubt that if one succeeds in getting a woman involved, she's more solid than a man... Once converted, women involve men, they involve their children.

Nardo Vanegas, communist and community leader, 2002.

class, from the 1950s onwards began active political work with the *juntas progresistas* (progressive committees). These urban neighborhood associations, designed to resolve local problems, assumed ever greater importance as the growth of cities and the expansion of public services under the control of autonomous public agencies generated new conflicts and opportunities.

The state responded to the politicizing of the juntas by founding the National Directorate of Community Development (DINADECO) in 1967. Public funds began to be channelled via this institution to community development associations. This weakened the juntas and successfully neutralized the Communist influence, since it was agents of the state who controlled the funds. The displacement of the Communists, however, was more complicated than expected, since the associations became a new site of competition between the Communists and their adversaries (principally Liberacionistas).

The growing Communist influence in the community organizations was favored by the 1952 founding of the Alliance of Costa Rican Women. Although the organization initially focussed on registering the new women citizens to vote, a right won in 1949, the Alliance soon dedicated itself to mobilizing working-class housewives to struggle at the community level, in particular against the unchecked rise in water and electricity rates. The strategy behind this campaign took its cue from the maternalist rhetoric of the first decades of the 20th century that insisted on the obligation of the wife and mother to oversee the welfare of her home. This kind of politicization of women reinforced rather than challenged traditional gender relations.

The incorporation of women contributed to the success of the protests, which showed that the conditions under which the state expanded were also defined, in part, by popular pressures and demands. The majority of the confrontations were resolved peacefully, with one exception: on 23 November 1962 a public protest of Cartago residents against what they considered an unjust charge on their electricity bills was brutally repressed by the police at a cost of three dead, dozens injured and almost thirty arrested after being savagely beaten. The government of Francisco Orlich (1962-66) tried to justify the repression by accusing the protesters of being Communists, but the attempt failed because the Cartago movement had a strong component of middle-class people and no Communist influence.

On top of the protests and community mobilizations, Costa Rica was shaken-up by a variety of social conflicts during the long boom years.

Cover of *Our Voice*, the newspaper of the Alliance of Costa Rican Women: *The time has come for women to join together in defense of peace, land, and children!*, February 1967.

In the [Cartago] *hospital the scene that presented itself to the eyes of this journalist was something indescribable. Scenes of suffering; wounded on the benches, in the rooms, in the seats. The hospital medical staff worked frantically against time, trying to save lives... Hideous scenes. And hovering over it all a tremendous indignation.*

La Nación, 27 November 1962.

That entire period [from 1948] *up to 1970 was one of violence in the United* [Fruit Company zones]. *The only thing the Company didn't do was shoot us... I had a time when I practically lived in jails... We'd get on the train and the police would be there, we'd get off in some spot and the police would be waiting for us.*

José Meléndez Ibarra, union leader, 1981.

Between 1948 and 1954 the protests of urban artisans and workers, and those of banana laborers, were the most significant, as they bravely stood against the persecution of the post-Civil War period. Small and medium-sized coffee farmers mobilized in 1961 seeking to better regulate their relationship with the coffee processors. During the same period, the discontent of poor peasants began to assume a public form, sometimes through the organization of leagues and committees that had a leftward orientation.

The total number of rural squatter families (*precaristas*) grew from 14,000 in 1963 to 17,421 in 1973, and

The Gorillas, a poster in support of a banana workers's strike, by the Student Federation of the University of Costa Rica, c. 1971.

2,203 struggles over land flared up between 1963 and 1970, most of them in Guanacaste, the Pacific south and Limón province (areas in which ranches and banana plantations were expanding). The state met this and other similar challenges by creating specialized agencies devoting attention to specific social problems. The desire to deal with popular discontent through legal and peaceful means, which had predominated in the Central Valley since the eighteenth century, culminated almost two hundred years later in a complex and diverse array of institutions.

The objective of these agencies was to brake the momentum of popular mobilizations. To achieve this efficiently, they had to address popular demands to some degree. This dynamic led to different collective actors taking on a corporate character – that is, forming themselves into co-operatives, associations, juntas, unions, boards, leagues, professional societies and the like – in order to lobby the state more effectively.

The unequal distribution of prosperity had a very visible geographical dimension. The urban world (with San José by far the most prominent center) concentrated 42 percent of the populace in 1973. It boasted the best services, infrastructure and income, but these advantages came at the expense of the rural areas. The Central Valley,

That job as an inspector [for Social Security] allowed him to get a close-up glimpse of a lot of misery... it made him very indignant. For example, in Naranjo [around 1963] a leading politician had a coffee beneficio with more than 200 women workers, but he refused to insure them. Among the workers were many single mothers who couldn't take their children to the Social Security hospital and who didn't have money for a doctor. Worse, they were afraid to even give their names to Jorge. They lived in real fear of losing their jobs. Finally he won the confidence of one of them, and she gave him all the names. And that's the way he got them all insured.

Margarita Salazar, the widow of poet Jorge Debravo, 1974.

We're from a really poor family. In Turrialba, we picked coffee and made baskets... Dad didn't have stable work... And so we came here, to San José... We came once, but we couldn't make it. We couldn't stick it out, and we went back. And later [in 1963] we came back again, and we've been here ever since: twenty-some years...

Driver with an import warehousing firm, c. 1988.

given its political and electoral weight, benefitted in proportionally greater terms from state investment than did Limón, Puntarenas and Guanacaste.

Urbanization was nourished by migration from the rural areas. A century earlier San José had bid farewell to those who set off to colonize the agricultural frontier. Now the city witnessed the return of their descendants. The process was limited outside the capital city, but San José experienced consistent growth. Aside from those who lived in the city proper, 500,000 people visited San José every day in 1976. The majority came from nearby communities, whose civic life dissipated as they became commuter suburbs. Although the growth of slums was still extremely limited as late as 1973, lack of planning meant that urban expansion would become chaotic. San José lost the European charm that had impressed the great Nicaraguan poet, Rubén Darío at the end of the 19th century, and was transformed into an ugly space, lacking in parks and facilities for pedestrians and cyclists, and with increasingly polluted rivers and air.

Rural culture still prevailed in 1950, but it was inexorably displaced by urban culture in a process linked to mass consumption. The opening of cinemas intensified. There was a notable widening in access to home appliances, especially the radio. The sale of records and comics expanded. And in 1960 television received its Costa Rican debut. Characteristic during this era was the growing penetration of news and entertainment coming from the United States, from the expressions of James Dean to the songs of Elvis Presley.

Locally-produced mass culture was concentrated in certain radio and television programs, particularly variety and game shows, and sportscasts. In the realm of popular music, orchestras like "Lubín Barahona and His Caballeros of Rhythm" began to share the terrain with rock groups. Football acquired a more entrepreneurial face with the construction of stadiums, better salaries for players and managers, and a more defined link with the world of advertising, radio and television.

Public transportation between the cities of San José and Alajuela, c. 1950s.

By and large, the University of Costa Rica (UCR) was ideologically conservative, and oriented towards training the technicians and professionals demanded by the public sector and Liberación Nacional. Nevertheless, the UCR provided a milieu for experimentation in theater, dance and visual arts (in 1953 Margarita Bertheau held the country's first exhibition of abstract art). The state also supported the arts by creating a series of prizes, awards and cultural agencies. The process culminated in the founding of a Ministry of Culture, Youth and Sports in 1971.

Schiller's *María Estuardo* at the University Theater, September 1975.

An official culture was institutionalized through state support between 1950 and 1970. There was a notable quantitative increase in literary and artistic production, but much of it lacked originality. The exceptions to this were works created by artists whose formative years preceded 1948: the painters, Francisco Amighetti and Manuel de la Cruz González; the sculptors, Juan Manuel Sánchez and Francisco Zúñiga; and the novelists, Joaquín Gutiérrez and Fabián Dobles. The most significant writers to emerge after 1950 were the poet Jorge Debravo (1938-67) and Luisa González (1904-99), who in 1970 published her brilliant and autobiographical novella, *A Ras del Suelo* (*Dirt Poor*).

Dominated by the values of Central Valley society, the educational and cultural policies strengthened the national identity invented by Liberals in the 1880s, whose emphasis was on "white" Costa Rica. The model was imposed on communities of indigenous and mulatto descent settled in Guanacaste and Puntarenas, but it had its greatest impact on the black population of Limón. The period after 1950 saw the gradual assimilation of a once distinctive, anglophone West Indian culture into the dominant Hispanic mode. This process, which led to the decadence of an active and cosmopolitan public sphere created by Afro-Caribbean immigrants in the first three decades of the 20th century, was fomented by people from the highlands who settled in the zone (attracted by

By then we were in the 1940s, and black men and women were still the majority [in Limón]. *But then white migration began... And shortly after that the boom in nationalist policies began, seeking to marginalize all Afro-Caribbean cultural expression, the language, the religion, the lodges, dance, music... We suffered a dreadful cultural imperialism from the interior of the country.*

Afro-Costa Rican poet Eulalia Bernard, October 2005.

land for colonization and by a new boom in the banana industry), by racism, and by the state's refusal to offer English instruction in public schools.

The Cold War context determined the cultural climate of the years 1950-70. The cosmopolitanism and intellectual openness characteristic of Costa Rica's urban actors during the Liberal era (1870-1930), were destroyed by the rabid anti-Communism of print, radio and television media controlled by a small circle of wealthy families; by the moral conservatism of middle classes bedazzled by prosperity; and by a rebound in Church influence in public life. The ecclesiastical hierarchy distanced itself from the social commitment that had distinguished the Church during the 1940s, and stood against the "option for the poor" endorsed by the Second Vatican Council (1962-65) and the Episcopal Conference of Medellin (1968).

The Costa Rican novel of most prestige outside the country, Carlos Luis Fallas' *Mamita Yunai*, was tacitly prohibited inside the country between 1950 and 1970 because of its revolutionary character. The ideological asphyxia and cultural torpor began to abate after 1967, in the heat of Latin America's guerrilla struggles and the emergence of the student movement throughout the West.

In Costa Rica the origin of student unrest was more cultural than political.

From the death of Sanabria [in 1952] *up until the beginning of the 1980s the Catholic Church in Costa Rica has not undertaken a single initiative in the social and political life of the country. It has, however, consolidated its privileged position to provide religious instruction in public educational establishments, to enjoy financing from the public treasury... to endow itself with costly temples and magnificent rectories, and to be included in every act of state protocol and in the inauguration of public and private works.*

Javier Solís, former priest, 1983.

It was accompanied by a drug culture in some university circles, and even among high school students (especially those who attended private high schools). But drug consumption was only a small part of a wider process that gave rise to an intellectual vanguard whose typical symbols were blue jeans, beards and long hair.

Costa Rican youth radicalism went beyond love of the Beatles and the Catalan singer, Joan Manuel Serrat. On the 24th of April 1970 thousands of high school and university students stoned the Legislative Assembly in a protest against mining concessions given to the transnational company, ALCOA.

The cry of "ALCOA NO!" was the beginning of a more profound and

The 24th of April 1970 in San José.

On June 25th, 1971, at eleven at night [in San José], *I was forced into a jeep without license plates by five men in plain clothes... They took me, like a criminal, to the Second Company, where they proceeded to do an inventory of my belongings... They confiscated photographs... of the riots of June 1st* [resulting from a march of university students in solidarity with banana workers] *in which some of us were being attacked by the police... The following morning... three of them started to beat me... and they screamed... «Bust his miserable life. That's how we're going to break these students».*

Alfonso Chase, poet, July 1971.

violent intellectual radicalization than that of the turn of the century. Although the organized left did not know how to take advantage of this, the swing towards radical stances led to a critique of the Costa Rica constructed by Liberación Nacional. Governments tried to defuse the criticism by devoting significantly more resources to health and education. The new left also enriched the cultural life of the country, which witnessed a few golden years between 1970 and 1978.

The governments of José Figueres (1970-74) and Daniel Oduber (1974-78) provided a stage where dance, theater and classical music could flourish. The output of publishers, painters, sculptors and documentary filmmakers also increased. Of most importance, higher education expanded with the founding of three new public universities: the Universidad Nacional Autónoma, the Instituto Tecnológico de Costa Rica (concentrating on technology-related education) and the Universidad Estatal a Distancia (concentrating on extension services). Meanwhile a community of highly-skilled scientists and professionals was consolidated thanks to an active program of scholarships to promote post-graduate studies, especially in the United States and Europe.

The social and cultural splendor of the 1970s was shaken by the sudden rise in the price of oil in 1973, at the same time that the Central American

Common Market exhausted its capacity for growth and the price paid for agricultural exports dropped. The full brunt of the crisis, however, was postponed by a rise in the international price of coffee in 1976 and 1977 due to frost damage to the Brazilian crop.

Machinery in the Saprissa Textile Factory, San José, September 1977.

The ephemeral prosperity of the era disguised the actual demise of the dominant economic model. Agricultural diversification, intensified in the 1950s, had provided the revenues to finance industrialization after 1963. Consolidated in the context of the Alliance for Progress, the Costa Rican industrial sector came to be controlled by foreign capital, especially from the

US. The industry that arose was technology-intensive and failed to offer abundant employment. Although it benefitted from generous tax exemptions to introduce raw materials and machinery, the value of imports for industry outstripped that of industrial exports by 250 million dollars between 1966 and 1972 (not including profits repatriated to foreign investors).

The industrial sector had been converted into an elaborate apparatus for multiplying the value of foreign capital and transferring growing shares of the profits from the agricultural sector out of the country. Given these circumstances, the fiscal deficit sky-rocketed from half a million colones in 1950 to 90 million colones in 1970, and the foreign public debt grew from 29 million to 164 million dollars over the same two decades.

Long Live Independence. Newspaper cartoon. Hugo Díaz, September 1972.

State revenues depended on indirect taxes (customs and sales). Incapable of levying appropriate taxes on the wealthy, and unable to police tax evasion, governments chose to accumulate more debt.

The intense decapitalization of the economy provoked by industrialization was exacerbated by a pronounced growth in public spending over the 1970s. Since 1950 the state had dedicated itself to assisting in the accumulation of private capital; it now began to accumulate capital itself. Public investment in productive activities grew at an annual rate of 183 percent between 1974 and 1977.

The so-called "entrepreneur state", which defined the Oduber government, saw the Costa Rican Development Corporation (CODESA), founded in 1972, administering huge sums for public investment in an ambitious program of business creation in industry and agriculture. The result was that the state began to absorb credit that otherwise would have gone to the private sector. This caused important industrialists to shift their allegiance away from Liberación Nacional in the elections of 1978.

The creation of an "entrepreneur state" also helped to increase the foreign public debt enormously: from 164 million dollars in 1970 it had risen to just over one billion dollars in 1978. At the end of the 1970s the catastrophic

Initially the idea was to found a corporation... with the object of developing companies that, due to the magnitude of the investment required, could not be set up by the private sector, in order to get them up and running and then sell them to the private sector. The tendency changed during the government of Oduber. Instead of fomenting small-scale businesses, CODESA... embarked on a disproportionate number of very large ventures.

Walter Kissling, industrialist, November 1979.

costs of the post-war development model became evident with cruel suddenness: growth came screeching to a halt, and then Costa Rica seemed to move backwards in time as the creditors came knocking all at once and Nicaragua, El Salvador and Guatemala exploded in revolution.

President Rodrigo Carazo and his wife, Estrella Zeledón, in Sandinista Nicaragua, August 1980.

CHAPTER 10

RECENT PAST, NEAR FUTURE

Hit by a second oil shock, a sharp fall in coffee prices and soaring interest rates, the Costa Rican economy collapsed in 1980. The Gross Domestic Product (GDP) per capita, which had already started to drop in 1979, fell 10 percent in 1982. Over the course of that year, real salaries dropped a staggering 30 percent, unemployment rose to 9 percent and inflation shot up to 90 percent. The proportion of homes below the poverty line, which had fallen from 51 to 25 percent between 1961 and 1977, rose to 48 percent in 1982. The crisis was aggravated by regional devastation in 1983 when United Fruit closed down its operations in the Pacific south.

Workers protest in San José, c. 1981.

In 1978 and 1979 the people and government of Costa Rica had provided

The representative of the Fund arrived at my office [in January 1982]... *and took out his little sheet of paper, in a personal and private meeting... and he began to say that what was needed here was the suppression of public services... that we have to sacrifice education, popular nutrition... close hospital services... So I said to him: one moment, the only thing that's going to close here are the doors of this country to the likes of you* [because]... *you lack respect... for national sovereignty – so much so that you are going to leave within 48 hours!*

Ex-President Rodrigo Carazo, September 1986.

material, logistical and moral support to the Sandinista revolutionaries fighting to overthrow Nicaragua's Somoza dictatorship. After their triumph in July 1979 the Sandinistas moved to transform Nicaragua into a socialist country, while open revolutionary offensives were launched in El Salvador and Guatemala. Widespread warfare shattered regional trade and added one more challenge to the crisis facing Costa Rica: dealing with a growing influx of refugees and illegal aliens which brought 300,000 people by 1990.

The government of Rodrigo Carazo (1978-82) was initially dominated by *neoliberalismo*, Latin America's version of ultra-free market conservatism, but its erratic economic policy deepened the crisis. In search of loans to keep the industrial sector afloat and avoid social chaos, the Carazo administration signed two agreements with the International Monetary Fund (IMF), and broke each one in short order.

The "recommendations" of the IMF included privatizing state enterprises, reducing public sector employment and social spending, eliminating subsidies on basic foodstuffs, and other measures from the free market playbook. Given the revolutionary Central American context that was impinging on the country, the counsel of the IMF was considered suicidal. In September 1981 the Carazo government declared a moratorium on the country's foreign debt and in January 1982 it broke off all negotiations with the IMF and expelled its representatives from the country.

This did not solve the debt crisis. Costa Rica's foreign public debt reached $3.7 billion in 1985, and between 1983 and 1988 servicing that debt ate up 29 percent of the total value of exports. Despite the severity of the economic crisis, Costa Rica's political system did not collapse. The Partido Liberación Nacional (PLN) won the next election, and the new President, Luis Alberto Monge (1982-86) had a clear message for the US administration of Ronald Reagan, which was intently waging a proxy war on the Sandinista revolution: if they

Ronald Reagan and Luis Alberto Monge at the White House, November 1982.

Costa Rican support is a critical factor in developing broad-based domestic and international support for U.S. Central American policy. Both because of our shared values, and to preserve Costa Rica as a model of democratic development for the region, a primary U.S. interest and objective is the preservation of Costa Rican democracy. Recent economic failure has called into question, for the first time in forty years, the ability of the democratic system to respond to the legitimate aspirations of the Costa Rican people. U.S. policy must therefore seek to achieve economic recovery in order to forestall Marxist-Leninist challenges.

USAID, March 1984.

wanted to use Costa Rica as a showcase to illustrate how capitalism and democracy could coexist in Central America, they had better start offering up some meaningful relief.

The United States Agency for International Development (USAID) was dispatched to Costa Rica, and Washington began to take measures to soften some conditions imposed by the IMF. In the process, however, USAID was transformed into a parallel Ministry of Finance and the release of funds was still contingent on the Costa Rican government meeting demands of international financial organizations. Prices charged for public services were raised, public spending was reduced and so were levies on imports (which by and large came from the US). The privatization of state enterprises got underway (especially subsidiaries of CODESA), and non-traditional exports were encouraged. Private banks got a boost, and their number grew from 11 to 24 between 1984 and 1996. Washington backed this process by approving the Caribbean Basin Initiative, an agreement that allowed a wide variety of Central American products to enter the United States free of duties.

USAID transferred nearly 1.3 billion dollars to Costa Rica between 1982 and 1990, and understandably garnered powerful allies in business and political circles. The majority of these funds were channeled outside the purview of the Auditor General's office or the Legislative Assembly. The disbursement was carried out by private organizations, among the most important being the Costa Rican Coalition for Development Initiatives (CINDE). Because of the influence they wielded, these entities were dubbed the "parallel state".

The new economic direction provoked a struggle between social democrats and neoliberals within the PLN. Starting in 1984, the neoliberals gained the ascendancy. The political opposition backed the transformation initiated by the Monge government in return for changes in electoral laws. A reform was approved in December 1982 allowing the leaders of the Unity Coalition (which had given Carazo the presidency in 1978) to found the Social Christian Unity Party (PUSC) without losing the right to state financing. So began the era of two-party politics in Costa Rica.

A change in model and the extra outside funding (mainly from the US) helped to stabilize the economy by 1982-83. The number of strikes dropped from an annual average of 29 between 1979 and 1981, to 12 from 1982 to 1985. Still, cutbacks to social spending (from 23 to 14 percent of GDP between 1980 and 1982) and huge increases in the cost of public services led to a new wave of popular

The monies of the U.S. contributors come to the Costa Rican state [via USAID] *but a mechanism is invented whereby they do not actually enter the state coffers, and they remain beyond the grasp of the Legislative Assembly, the Executive, and the Auditor General... A series of institutions are created, and nobody knows who they belong to or who controls them... There are subsidies for creating private banks, there are donations, there are low-interest loans to promote certain activities, but for the bean farmers there are no subsidies, because that would produce a fiscal deficit.*

John Biehl, Advisor to President Óscar Arias Sánchez, June 1988.

mobilization with deep community backing. These protests, which became quite intense between 1983 and 1985, succeeded in getting the Monge government to introduce the price increases on services (electricity and water) in a gradual manner, but the protesters got no institutional response to their public housing demands.

The Reagan administration hoped to convert Costa Rican territory into a southern front in its counter-revolutionary war on Sandinista Nicaragua. Nicaraguan exiles began to operate in San José, sponsored by a US Embassy that had seized effective control over Costa Rica's security forces and given them a military orientation. The main local print, radio and television news media were loyal allies of the US strategy,

Peace march in San José, 15 May 1984.

roundly calling for a militarization of Costa Rica to confront the red menace of Sandinismo and crack down on local underground ultra-leftists who perpetrated a series of violent actions between 1980 and 1983.

The Costa Rican government accepted all but one of Washington's demands: it would not agree to "invite" US troops to establish bases in Costa Rica. The pressure became intolerable, and in 1983 Monge played his last card. He invoked the symbolic weight of Costa Rican history and declared the country's neutrality. He received massive popular support. In 1984 a gigantic march for peace wound its way through the streets of San José, affirming national sovereignty and strengthening the calls for a diplomatic solution to the Central American conflict.

The PLN won the vote in 1986 and the new government of Óscar Arias (1986-90) launched a vigorous popular housing program to reduce the political clout of the community activists. At the same time, Arias deepened the neoliberal policy direction of government, slashing state assistance to agricultural producers who supplied the internal market. This drew strong protests from them. Although they could not stop the changes, big and middling farmers did succeed in negotiating longer adjustment periods and better conditions to adapt to the new context. In contrast to

[T]*hese* [poor] *farmers vegetate on the agricultural frontier... they satisfy the politicians' romantic belief that the country lives a democracy based on small agrarian property...* [An option for solving the problem of this sector would be] *to transform, as happened in the Central Valley, the small and marginal producer into a wage worker with a relatively good, stable salary and with better public services (education, health)...*

President of the Central Bank, Eduardo Lizano, 1986.

[We protest] *the situation of impoverishment and annihilation that we have been suffering for a great many years... a structure of unmanageable costs... taxes and direct charges levied on producers... a total lack of technical help, unjust conditions of production and marketing... all in order to maintain intolerable subsidies and benefits for industrialists.*

Letter sent to President Óscar Arias Sánchez by peasant leaders, September 1986.

this, the disappearance of the peasantry – a trend that had been slowed by the crisis of 1980 – intensified: peasants fell from 14 to 7 percent of the Economically Active Population between 1984 and 2000.

The peace card was the ace in the foreign policy of the new government. Arias succeeded in brokering a peace plan that was signed by the five leaders of Central America. The Costa Rican initiative sought to undermine Washington pressure to militarize the country, while reestablishing the regional trade. Arias was able to outmaneuver a US administration obsessed with defeating the Sandinistas militarily, and in 1987 he was awarded the Nobel Peace Prize.

This honor was one of two spectacular Costa Rican interventions on

Peasants and farmers opine about the economic policies of the Arias government, San José, September 1986.

the international stage. The second was the brilliant performance of the national soccer team in the 1990 World Cup, held in Italy. The team of semi-professional players of working-class origin defeated Scotland (1-0) and Sweden (2-1) to advance to the second round. The nation erupted in jubilant celebration.

As the excitement of the Nobel Prize and soccer glory dissipated, Costa Ricans woke up to a new geopolitical reality. The success of the peace plan, the electoral defeat of the Sandinistas in 1990, the collapse of the Soviet Union and the crisis of the Western left all meant that Washington completely lost interest in Central America. US aid to Costa Rica fell abruptly from 78 million to 20 million dollars between 1990 and 1992. After closing down operations in San José in 1996, USAID was substituted the same year by CR-USA, a neoliberal-oriented foundation that used leftover monies from previous USAID funds.

Compensating for the drop in aid was a dizzying rise in direct foreign investment. From an average of (US) $55 million annually between 1982 and 1986, investment from abroad jumped to $132 million annually between 1987 and 1991, then to an average of $307 million per year between 1992 and 1996, and more recently to $542 million a year between 1997 and 2004. These resources

There will be no lasting peace in Central America without democracy... The many problems of injustice, exploitation and misery that confront the region stem from the refusal of the oligarchic groups to cede their privileges... There are people here [in Costa Rica]... *who do not believe in a peaceful solution..., who wish the war to continue regardless of the consequences..., who have never worn out their shoes because they've spent their lives on their knees...: a very intolerant minority of the extreme right who are the ones that... write in the media..., who are the ones who generate those editorials in* La Nación.

President Óscar Arias, October 1987.

March demanding govern-
ment funding for public universities, October 1986.

*We had to put the prob-
lem right, and that
meant cuts in public
spending, an adjustment
of tariffs... [taking] very
tough measures... a rise
in the sales tax to
13%... a reduction in
the number of public
sector employees... It
was painful for me to
dismiss 700 people from
the railway...*

President Rafael Ángel Calderón Fournier, March 1991.

tended to be directed toward tax-ex-
empt business activities that did not
help increase the central government's
taxation revenues (between 1984 and
1990 they declined from 13 to 11 percent of GDP).

The first PUSC government
(1990-94) was led by Rafael Ángel
Calderón Fournier, the son of the great
social reformer, Calderón Guardia.
"Junior" took advantage of the rising
government deficit to justify an even
stronger neoliberal program. Among
other things, this so-called "shock therapy" involved a sales tax increase from
10 to 13 percent, salary freezes, budget
cuts and a reduction in public employment (through layoffs with severance
packages and the beginning of the clo-
sure of the national railroads, which
were partially revived in 2006). Education, health, and housing expenditures
diminished from 17 to 15 percent of
GDP between 1989 and 1992. The effect of this reduction was soon visible
in the reappearance of diseases that had
formerly been eradicated and in a rise
in informal employment, student drop-
out rates and households living below
the poverty line (which grew from 27 to
32 percent between 1990 and 1991).

Workers responded to this "therapy" with 89 strikes and stoppages between 1990 and 1993, of which 75
were led by public employees. Criticism from the Catholic Church also
eroded implementation of the new

economic policy, and state universities stymied the attempt to cut their budgets. Popular pressure forced the government to abandon the original plan which, together with an economic recovery, reduced the proportion of families living in poverty. Between 1994 and 2005, on average, one in five families was poor.

José María Figueres Olsen took advantage of the profound discontent provoked by the first PUSC government. The PLN presidential candidate, and son of José Figueres Ferrer, waged a campaign based on the promise of returning to pre-1978 policies. Once in power, however, his government (1994-98) applied "shock therapy" more violent than that of Calderón Fournier.

In 1994 the Costa Rican state employed 15 percent of the work force (a proportion that had declined only slightly since 1979). It controlled the equivalent of 60 percent of GDP and it held a monopoly on insurance, electricity, fuel refining and telecommunications. Faced with a government deficit equal to 5 percent of GDP, in April 1995 Figueres Olsen signed a pact with Calderón Fournier (still the leader of the PUSC) to deepen state "reform".

The pact was soon judged illegitimate by the majority of the citizenry because it involved dismantling the welfare state built between 1940 and

Jesus entrusted to us the loving care of the poor, who in our country represent more than 70% of the total population... As a Pastor I am troubled by the excessive rise in the cost of living, a consequence of taxes that hit the least protected classes of the country hardest. In the name of the poor of my country and with the greatest of respect I entreat the government, when the time comes to raise taxes, to keep in mind the principles of fair taxation according to which those who have the most are those who must pay the most, so that those who have less might pay less.

Román Arrieta, Archbishop of San José, criticizes the "shock therapy" of the government of Calderón Fournier, August 1990.

1978 by the very fathers of the signatories, Calderón Guardia and Figueres Ferrer. The civic coalition opposed to the pact organized vast popular mobilizations in July and August of 1995, with a strong showing from teachers and professors who had been hurt by a reform of their pension plans. The protests culminated in a violent attack on defenseless citizens by security forces trained by elite Chilean police (the *carabineros*).

The movement was not able to stop legislative approval of the pension reform, but it did brake the privatization of public institutions. These protests also spelled the end of the political

March against the reform of the pension laws, August 1995.

elite's strategy of negotiating structural adjustment programs with the IMF and World Bank in order to claim later that the institutional and economic transformation of Costa Rica they sought was really the result of a prior agreement that they had no power to question.

The PUSC returned to power with Miguel Ángel Rodríguez (1998-2002), who concentrated his energies on achieving a "national consensus" to privatize "state entities", most importantly the Costa Rican Electricity Institute (ICE). Dubbed the "ICE combo" in the parlance of the fast-food industry and backed by politicians who pointed for justification to the growing weight of the internal debt (which reached almost 27 percent of GDP in 1999), the project was violently rejected by the citizenry over March and April 2000. Spontaneous protests mushroomed into road blockages, work stoppages, and acts of civil disobedience that brought the country to a standstill and finally forced the government to withdraw its privatization plans indefinitely.

As the 1990s drew to a close it was clear just how much Costa Rica had changed since the crisis of 1980. In 1987, for the first time in 150 years the value of coffee and banana exports was surpassed, over a sustained period, by that of non-traditional exports. Principal among the new exports were textiles,

Teachers wounded... by kicks in the face... because they protested in defense of their pensions in front of the Presidential Mansion, while a sophisticated spying system directed from... that same mansion... intimidates... politicians and businessmen... Costa Rica is in ruins... Insincere promises of panaceas are made during election campaigns that are never fulfilled, withering the faith of the citizens in public institutions, while the great challenges facing the Republic are dealt with by means of secret pacts.

Fernando Guier E., lawyer, June 1996.

"The ICE is not for sale", March 2000.

President Oduber on a pineapple farm, c. 1976.

I sat in the front row, listening to this guy [a NASA official visiting Costa Rica c. 1967] *talk* [to high school students] *about rockets and rocket propulsion. He had copies of a booklet, 'So You Want To Be a Rocket Scientist,' by Wernher von Braun, it told you how to become a rocket scientist and work for NASA. That's what I wanted to do. That's when I formulated my plan to come to the United States.*

Franklin Chang, astronaut, 2003.

stitched together in maquiladoras (highly mobile, foreign-owned final assembly plants); pineapple production, an activity controlled by the transnational, Del Monte; ornamental plants; and seafood.

The export value of these and other similar products rose from 91 million to over 1.1 billion dollars between 1980 and 1995, and the growth of these exports helped to offset a drastic drop in the price of coffee between 1989 and 1993. By 2004 the value of non-traditional exports had reached 5.5 billion dollars, representing 87 percent of the total value of the country's exports. The phase of greatest increase in these non-traditional exports happened after 1996 when high-tech companies led by INTEL began to open plants in Costa Rica, taking advantage of the lower cost of infrastructure, the availability of public services, and the specialized skills of local workers.

Unlike other Central American states, Costa Rica has not experienced a massive exodus of people to the US and other industrialized countries over the last twenty-five years. Nevertheless, those who have departed, a large proportion of them professionals, still accounted for an additional source of dollars entering Costa Rica. The annual value of remittances rose from an average of $117.5 million between 1994 and 2000, to $256.6 million between 2001 and 2004. Of the $302 million remitted in 2004, over three-quarters came from the 45,269 Costa Ricans resident in the US.

The exceptional biodiversity of Costa Rica and the structure of parks and natural reserves (covering just over a quarter of the national territory in 2003) have provided the basis for the promotion of the country as an ideal destination for the eco-tourist from Europe, Canada and the United States in particular. The rapid growth in foreign tourism began in 1985, and it reached one million people in 1999. By 2004, almost 1.5 million tourists generated $1.3 billion in revenue and 7 percent of GDP.

In macroeconomic terms the results of new export industries are visible in

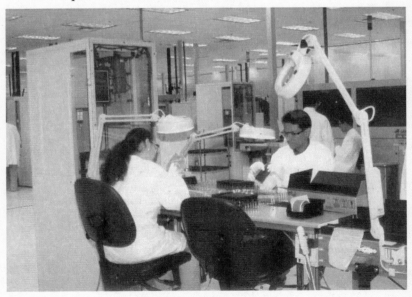

A work day at INTEL, c. 2000.

the GDP, which grew at an annual rate of 4 percent between 1987 and 2005. Critics point out that the most profitable operations are poorly integrated with the national economy, with their contribution concentrated in salaries and purchases from local suppliers. In 2000 INTEL's Costa Rican operation generated a commercial surplus of $900 million, of which only $200 million stayed in the country. Even so, despite its being a moderate proportion of the total profit, the lower sum still represented 74 percent of the total value of Costa Rican coffee exports in the same year.

An earlier style of promoting tourism in Costa Rica, 1938.

The ecological cost of the new economy has been uneven. The rate of deforestation reached 100,000 hectares per year between 1985 and 1988, the highest level in Central America, and one comparable to the destruction of the Amazon region during these same years. From 1989 to 1993, banana cultivation and ranching increased at the expense of the tropical forest. During the 1990s, however, greater controls on illegal logging and a variety of economic incentives allowed for some recuperation of forested areas. In 2001 forests covered almost half of Costa Rican territory, significantly greater than the roughly one-third recorded in 1977.

Tourist expansion has resulted in a certain ecological deterioration, especially in the coastal areas of the Caribbean and Guanacaste, and the new agricultural and industrial export activities have also increased levels of pollution. Nevertheless, the country's primary environmental problem is the chaotic urbanization of the Central Valley, an area that in 2005 hosted two-thirds of Costa Rica's 4.3 million people.

Stretching from Turrialba in the east to San Ramón in the west, this urban disaster is exemplified by the ever-expanding mall sprawl (whose fast food areas are the postmodern Tico's new forum) and the appearance of new housing developments on land that was once used for agriculture or forest. The growth of the suburbs and the closing of the railroads, combined with a reduction on import duties on

The charges... have not been denied, not by the Costa Rican Tourism Institute (ICT), not by the Ministry of Natural Resources, Energy and Mines (MIRENEM). They all accept that the damage [in Gandoca] *took place... [I had to] suffer in order to defend my house and the health of my children, I received death threats... Environmental destruction is unstoppable... The environmental policy of the Government* [of Calderón Fournier] *in this moment is a swindle...*

Ana Cristina Rossi, novelist, February 1993.

vehicles, stimulated a four-fold increase in the number of cars, trucks and buses in the country between 1985 and 2004, with the number of people per vehicle dropping from 11 to 4.5 over the course of these two decades.

The San Pedro Mall under construction in San José, November 1993.

The impact of the economic transformation in the work world has been broad and deep. Public sector employment shrank from 19 to 13 percent of the Economically Active Population between 1980 and 2003, despite the fact that more than 50 new state agencies were created during this period, in their majority linked to the neo-liberal model, and so juxtaposed to those created before 1978. Between 1985 and 2004, the population employed in the primary sector (mostly agriculture) dropped from over 27 to 15 percent, in the secondary sector (industry and construction) it languished at about 20 percent, and in the service sector it rose from half to almost two-thirds.

In the course of this redistribution, activities like construction, agriculture, private security and domestic service have been abandoned by Costa Ricans and taken up by immigrants, for the most part by the 300 to 400 thousand Nicaraguans who work legally and illegally in the country. The state's strategy to cope with this process has been a mix of persecution and expulsion of immigrants, massive legalizations (in 1990, 1993, and 1999), and a new immigration law, approved in 2005, that criminalizes all those involved in illegal immigrant trafficking.

Intense work days, abuse, instability, salaries below minimum wage (though still higher than those in the rest of Central America), and violations of work and human rights take a heavy toll on the illegal immigrants. Costa Rican workers have not been immune to a deterioration in their working conditions either, one quite visible in the maquiladoras. The typical middle class of the Golden Age of 1950-78, made up of professionals, public employees, teachers and small and middling farmers, has been supplemented by those in other more vulnerable and informal middle-class jobs connected to the expansion of the non-traditional export sector, trade, tourism, private banks

The cases of exploitation and abuse of workers continue to grow in the maquila industry... Unscrupulous entrepreneurs [reduce]... their costs by failing to comply with... obligations, like overtime pay, employer contributions to Social Security and others... In 28 companies... 194 infractions of the labor code were counted ...The majority of infractions involved... a failure to pay the minimum wage... and demands for illegal shifts of longer than 12 hours... Cases of sexual abuse were detected, as were incidents of the withholding of overtime pay and excessive reductions in the amount of break time...

La Nación, 31 December 1992.

Maquiladora workers, c. 1980s.

The Plan Martén is the great solution for heading off Communism... Moscow offers them [the workers] theories, while with the Plan Martén I offer them money. Let them decide between theories and money: I am certain that if they think, and if they want a future with economic security for their children, they will choose the "Solidarist" system... The basic reason behind my adoption of the system is that I want to get richer...

An entrepreneur with extensive coffee interests, 1954.

and new service activities like call centers and on-line gambling.

The deterioration in worker rights is related to the erosion of unions, and the decline of intellectual and political vanguards committed to social justice. Between 1984 and 2004 unions fell in number from 306 to 260 and the rate of unionization fell from 16 percent to 10 percent of the employed population. In contrast, "solidarist" associations grew from 832 with over 32,000 workers in 1986 to 1,212 in 2004 with almost 200,000 members. By the latter year they controlled funds totalling $2.1 billion.

Solidarismo is a form of labor organization based on contingency funds contributed by workers and owners in individual companies, which provide workers with some benefits and securities while sparing management the negotiating power of unions. First sponsored in 1947 by Alberto Martén, an associate of José Figueres, Solidarismo had a limited period of expansion in the 1950s. Thirty years later, however, in the midst of the economic crisis, it spread rapidly in the private sector, promoted by both business and government.

The rise of solidarismo, employer persecution, the state's anti-union policies, and conflicts among the unions themselves have all contributed to the collapse of the union movement. The erosion of trade unions was actually preceded by the crisis of the Costa Rican left, which destroyed itself in a series of internal conflicts beginning in 1982. This facilitated the offensive of the state and business against organized labor. The following period was characterized by a general loss of radicalism among intellectuals and politicians, who now began to ally themselves with their former opponents. Indeed, some people who were once prominent members of the left played key roles in the cabinets of Calderón Fournier and Figueres Olsen. The rise of neoliberalismo entailed the dismantling of the country's social and cultural vanguards forged in the political blast furnace of "ALCOA NO!"

In contrast to the deterioration in labor rights, civil rights have been

The left did not know how to cope with the specificity of our democracy... It died of electoral starvation... Nevertheless... the alternative of the left continues to be valid... While there are right-wing positions, one must continue to be on the left... While there is social injustice, one must... fight for change ...To be on the left is... to be against injustice, to dream of being able to build a better world... What matters now is to keep hope alive and not to allow us to be defeated in the realm of dreams..., dreams of a tomorrow that is better, more just, and freer for everyone...

Manuel Formoso, philosopher, February 1990.

[T]*he Constitutional Court has reminded Costa Ricans that the Political Constitution is not a dead letter filled with rhetoric but rather a living normative package that establishes the cardinal points at the political, social, and economic levels... [A] big problem for constitutional justice is that public employees don't understand what they cannot do... what the Constitutions does not want them to do, and that rebelling against or disobeying the authority of the constitutional tribunal is rebellion or disobedience against the Constitution itself... [I]n Costa Rica the average judge really hesitates to question the authorities on laws: the attitude is to defend the law and not the Constitution.*

Rodolfo Piza Escalante, Constitutional Court judge, 1992.

reinforced. In 1989 a special constitutional court, the Sala Cuarta was established, and 1992 saw the creation of an official ombudsperson, the Defensoría de los Habitantes. Moreover, the state began to undertake programs to enhance the lot of specific segments of the population, with attention to geographic, ethnic, gender, and age differences, and also to people with disabilities.

An unexpected result of the strengthening of civil rights was that the Sala Cuarta, invested with the power to annul decisions made by the Legislature and the Executive, was in some cases able to limit the economic and institutional reform of the country promoted by the neoliberals. At the end of 1987 the Arias government granted a concession to a transnational corporation (Comcel-Millicom) to exploit cellular telephony in the country, but the contract was declared unconstitutional by the Sala Cuarta in October 1993 in response to a suit filed by ICE workers. In April 2000, the Sala annulled the legislative approval in first reading given to the so-called "Combo ICE". This new judicial power contributed to making the transformation process gradual and reduced its social impact. Democracy also limited structural reform, since it could be electorally beneficial to assume anti-neoliberal platforms, a position that has been the basis for the emergence of new political parties.

The reinforcement of civil rights and the emphasis on the individual were part of a wider change in cultural and educational policies. The Carazo government was the first to declare that the financing of culture (especially high culture) must depend on the market. Indeed a market in plastic art has appeared, particularly in painting. Other manifestations of this process include the private sponsorship of theater festivals, classical music performances and other artistic activities. The same dynamic was behind the filming of eight Costa Rican feature films between 1984 and 2004: *La Segua, Los Secretos de Isolina, Eulalia, Asesinato en El Meneo, Password, Mujeres Apasionadas, Marasmo* and *Caribe.*

Education was not exempt from this drift toward the marketplace. In 1980 barely more than one percent of primary schools were private, but by 2004 the proportion was reaching one in 13. The proportion of private high schools went from 12 to 30 percent during the same period, while the number of private universities shot up from 1 to 50. In 2004 some 87,000 students paid $104 million annually to train at these universities, many of which lack laboratories, libraries and specialized academic personnel.

In 2005 Costa Rica had roughly 166,000 university students, making up 4 percent of the total population (in 1967, by contrast, they barely represented half a percent). The increase helps to explain why Costa Ricans have abandoned certain occupations, why the country offers attractive skilled labor for high-tech industries, and why new generations of technicians, professionals, and intellectuals no longer depend on the expansion of the state, but on that of the market.

Privatization has also advanced in the health sector, with the opening of private clinics and hospitals, and in the area of security. In 1995 the country had only 8,629 national police, while 121 different companies employed 9,089 security guards. In 2004 the difference was greater still: 9,825 public cops and 12,692 private ones.

Teatro Chic (movie theater) in Alajuela, c. 1960s, today part of a bank.

An identification with the private has been reinforced by cultural transnationalization. The rapid penetration of the "American way of life" was assisted by the introduction of cable television in 1981 and subsequently by Internet access; by the founding of private primary and secondary schools that emphasize the teaching of English; by the boom in advertising agencies whose styles are copied from Miami; and by the opening of video arcades and video rental shops. Cinema was one of the victims of this transformation. Between 1980 and 1995, dozens of rural and urban movie houses closed their doors, and in those that remained or were built anew in the malls, screens were monopolized by US distributors (with the important exception of the Sala Garbo).

Cultural globalization has also been fueled by the tourist boom, by greater access to products from other countries made available by liberalized trade policies, and by immigration, especially from Nicaragua. Globalizing cultural trends have also been assisted by the expansion of evangelical Protestantism, whose devotees more than tripled in number between 1978 and 1986 (from 50 thousand to over 150 thousand believers). In 1990, about 10 percent of Costa Ricans attended evangelical services at least occasionally, a proportion that stabilized at around 16 percent in 2002. The evangelical message, for the

I bought a pressure cooker and a rice cooker from the door-to-door salesman on the payment plan. Five hundred colones [about $3.60] a week is nothing... In December the missus told me that she wanted a washing machine. I asked for some vacation pay at work, kicked in some of the Christmas bonus and went shopping at the Alto de Guadalupe. I saw they were selling one on a corner. I asked the woman how much it was. She told me 15,000 colones [$107] because it was used. Exactly what I had in my pocket.

Construction worker, 1993.

most part a conservative one, is propagated by US-based missions whose numbers doubled between 1965 and the end of the 1970s.

The success of the evangelicals revealed that the Catholic Church had been left behind by social and cultural change (the nominally Catholic population declined from 90 to 76 percent between 1985 and 2002). This was due in part to the status of Catholicism as the official religion of the state, a condition that ensures ecclesiastical officials receive privileges and subsidies while it co-opts their words and deeds. Although the Catholic Church tried to deepen its commitment to the poor after 1970, and particularly during the worst years of the economic crisis, its success was limited. The

Holy Week, March 1985.

Church has also been hurt by sexual abuse scandals involving assaults on minors by priests, and by corruption scandals.

The Catholic Church's loss of influence was closely related to greater secularization in society, one evident in demographic data. The total size of the family fell from 7 to 2 children between 1960 and 2005. These smaller families were increasingly headed by a woman: between 1987 and 2003 alone female-headed households grew from one in six to one in four. The divorce rate grew astronomically starting in 1990, when 15 percent of marriages ended this way, and by 2004 the figure rose to 41 percent of marriages. Illegitimacy also rose enormously from 39 to 59 percent of total births over the same years.

This change in family structure means that Costa Rica currently has more people of working age than people in dependent conditions (those under 15, or over 65). The process of demographic transition is also related to growing feminine participation in the labor force: from one-fifth to one-third between 1973 and 2005. New spaces for women were opened in the professions, in business, in politics and the arts during the 1980s and 1990s. Currently the most important Costa Rican literary figures are women: the novelist, Tatiana Lobo, the poet and actress, Ana Istarú, and

Banana workers, December 1992.

Ana Cristina Rossi, author of *La Loca de Gandoca* (1992), a novel about tourism and environmental damage on the Caribbean coast.

In the 1980s a feminist movement began to take shape, made up of professionals and intellectuals, and concentrating on the struggle against domestic abuse and gender inequities, especially among women who participated in politics or who worked in the public sector. In 1997 the movement won passage of a reform that obliged political parties to fill at least 40 percent of their eligible posts with women. This resulted in the proportion of women deputies in the Legislature rising from 12 to 39 percent between 1986 and 2006, and that of women city councilors going from 6 to 40 percent. In contrast, the feminist movement has avoided getting involved in the systematic defense of working women's rights.

The backdrop to this lack of interest is a consolidation of class culture. Status is increasingly associated with the consumption of name-brand products and access to private services, especially in education, health, and security. Class distinction is expressed in its strongest form in residential segregation. Prior to 1980 the prevalent model of city life involved the sharing of space, even if unequally. This has been replaced by a model that separates the popular sectors from the middle classes and the business and political elites.

They keep a record of when we get our period so they can ask for a urine sample and see whether we're pregnant. Sometimes they ask to see our sanitary napkin. You feel so humiliated when the doctor does this. They give us sick leave when the doctor decides it — in other words, never — and you don't have any way to fight for your rights because they don't give you time off to go to the Social Security clinic. Government work inspectors? Don't make me laugh. We only put up with this because we need the work.

Maquiladora worker, 1995.

While the proportion of homes beneath the poverty line has stabilized at 20 percent, inequality is increasing. According to the most recent census of 2000, 77 percent of Costa Ricans own their own homes, and over 80 percent of homes have potable water, electricity, colored television, refrigerator and washing machine. By contrast, in 2004 the Gini coefficient (a calculation that measures inequality on a scale of 0 to 1, with 0 being the most equal) rose to 0.4750, well above the 0.3577 reached in 1988.

The segregation characteristic of urban expansion at the end of the 20th century, in a context of diminishing public security, has contributed to a change in the nature of crime. Although some youth gangs flourished during the 1990s, they did not reach the size or the degree of organization of the fearsome "maras" of Guatemala, El Salvador and Honduras. Nevertheless, the criminal world has professionalized itself, in terms of arms, strategies and links with elected officials, executives and lawyers.

The influence of organized crime is visible in the creation of networks of female and male prostitution of adults and minors (for the most part, servicing tourists, the subject of the 2002 film, *Password*), and in the operation of teams specializing in bank robberies, auto thefts, and even paid hits. One of their victims was Parmenio Medina, a

A girlfriend from the barrio introduced me to some men and she explained what I had to do, later I became the girlfriend of a cabbie, we're done now, but he's really good with me, he introduces me to men, sometimes he brings me to the motels himself, when they're foreigners, like gringos, between the two of us we make good money.

Young woman of 17, c. 2001.

I've smoked marijuana everywhere, even in the sewers of San José. When we lived in Desamparados, I became a real head. I used to get together with this chick, she was a total operator, but really hot. One time we broke into a house and the police caught us. We were arrested. Now I don't smoke marijuana in the street because the next thing you know you're busted. A few people get together, things start getting a bit crazy and the police arrive.

Construction worker, 1992.

Old age and poverty, c. 2005.

journalist of Colombian origin assassinated in 2001 for denouncing serious irregularities in the operations of a Catholic radio station.

Costa Rican identity was constructed on the basis of its ability to imagine Costa Ricans as a nation of white, peaceful, secure, egalitarian, rural, and peasant people oriented toward the search for social justice. At the beginning of the 21st century Costa Ricans find themselves a pluricultural and multi-racial country, urbanized, lacking security, increasingly differentiated and acquiring greater levels of competitiveness and consumption. The resulting identity crisis, evident in the pessimism and uncertainty that Costa Ricans show in opinion polls, has combined with the growing discontent of a significant part of the population with increasing social inequality and corruption.

Injustices in the tax system are a key component of the inequality: between 1990 and 2004 the taxation revenues of the central government barely grew from 11 to 13 percent of GDP (a level similar to that of 1984). After five fiscal reforms effected during this period, the weight of income tax only rose from 14 to 24 percent of central government's taxation revenues. On top of this, the treasury is strongly affected by tax evasion, which is estimated at between a minimum of 3 and a maximum of 10 percent of

GDP (between half a billion and 1.5 billion dollars per year).

Tax fraud is the rule rather than the exception: corruption has been an inherent part of the neoliberal transformation. Political venality was limited during the Liberal era, but it widened (and deepened) in line with the growth of the state after 1948, and reached unprecedented dimensions starting in the 1980s in step with neoliberal ideology's attack on the welfare state, and on state controls over economic activity.

All too many politicians and business people have used their political, business and family connections to increase their wealth through contraband, influence peddling, patronage, and the embezzlement of funds from state banking institutions. The most notorious example of this new style of super-corruption during the 1990s was associated with the Certificates of Tax Deferral (CATs), implemented to foment non-traditional exports – an incentive that led some entrepreneurs to create shell export firms that claimed tax rebates on bogus export receipts. The state transferred one billion dollars in CATs to a variety of companies, including some transnational corporations, between 1984 and 1999.

Speculative ventures, irregularities in loan concessions and misappropriation of funds led to the 1994 collapse of the Banco Anglo Costarricense following the discovery of losses totaling

With all the money that they've robbed how many houses they could have built for so many poor people!

Resident of Desamparados, October 2004.

The Commission proved that, just like in other countries, Costa Rica is witnessing the penetration of narco-trafficking into state institutions, into banking institutions and into many other public activities, with the object of procuring influence and, where necessary, assistance in the transhipment of drugs or the laundering of money.

Costa Rican Legislative Assembly, Second Report of the Commission on Drug Trafficking, July 1989.

$54.5 million. The closing of the institution (the oldest in the country, founded in 1863) left over 1,700 people unemployed. The costs of the collapse, underwritten by the state, were more than would have been the case had the administration chosen to recapitalize the bank: the central government's public debt rose by almost 10 percent of GDP between 1994 and 1996 (a rise that was later used as an excuse to justify a further sale of state assets).

The corruption that took shape during the 1980s was soon shown to have links to the criminal world. The outbreak of revolutions in Central America introduced arms trafficking, which was the prelude to the trafficking of narcotics on a vast scale. Among

Protest march of employees against the closing of the Banco Anglo Costarricense, 13 September 1994.

the leading promoters of both activities were US government personnel (those of the CIA in particular) who relied on drug trafficking in order to pay for their illegal arms supplies to the anti-Communist Contra guerrillas fighting in Nicaragua.

The Irangate scandal was quickly forgotten, but the Colombian cartels, in search of safe sites for drug transshipment and opportunities for money laundering, achieved a deep penetration of Costa Rica's political, business and professional groups. In 1997, 63 firms were investigated for supposedly using CATs to expedite the laundering of profits from the international drug trade. US officials in charge of losing the expensive, vicious, and utterly ineffective "war on drugs" calculated that in 1990 a minimum of 12 tons of cocaine entered the United States via Costa Rica each year; by 1997 their calculation was 50 tons, and by 2001 some 70 tons.

The impact of corruption was enormous in a political system in which the disappearance of ideological differences between the PLN and the PUSC had left party identities and loyalties in crisis. The growing disenchantment of the citizens with politics was expressed at the ballot box. Voter turnout fell from an average of 81 percent between 1962 and 1994 to 70 percent in 1998. In the latter year, the proportion of presidential and congressional votes captured

We can trust that justice will be done: 53% of those polled are in disagreement with the statement. Deputies make laws to enrich themselves: 76% agree. The government robbed the teachers' pensions: 50% agree... Government propaganda is designed to deceive the people: 82% agree. The current policies of the Government are increasing poverty: 84% agree. Campaign promises are a political swindle: 88% agree.

Opinions of Costa Ricans, from the University of Costa Rica's Annual National Poll, September 1996.

Employers give their workers time off to rally for CAFTA, October 2005.

I think the only way to [overturn the prohibition on presidential reelection] is a constitutional reform in the Legislative Assembly. The Constitutional Court doesn't have anything to do with this. It would be mocking 57 deputies if you avoided a debate in Parliament. It would be totally anti-democratic to knock on the doors of the Judiciary.

Óscar Arias, December 1999.

by the PLN and the PUSC combined were only 92 and 76 percent, compared to the 98 and 87 percent on average attained between 1986 and 1994.

In 2002 participation dropped even more to under 70 percent, and the PLN and the PUSC together scarcely captured 70 percent of the presidential vote, and 57 percent of the congressional vote. With no party attaining 40 percent of the valid vote necessary for winning the presidency on a first ballot, for the first time in the history of Costa Rica the election went to a second round, won finally by the PUSC candidate, Abel Pacheco. During his government (2002-06) the neoliberals used a new strategy to foment the privatization of state assets. They took advantage of the negotiations for a Central American Free Trade Agreement (CAFTA) between the US, Central America, and the Dominican Republic, to include at the last minute as part of the agreement the "opening" of a number of public services to private sector competition, in particular insurance and telecommunications.

The deep division provoked by the negotiating of CAFTA was complicated by peculiarities in the 2005-06 electoral campaign. Due to a controversial decision of the Constitutional Court in 2003, Óscar Arias was allowed to run again for the presidency (presidential re-election had been prohibited in 1969), and this provoked a deep split in the PLN. In 2004, investigations by the media revealed irregularities associated with a Finnish loan for $39.5 million for the purchase of medical equipment and other dubious exchanges of influence for money related to the acquisition of 400,000 cellular telephone lines from a French company. The charges involved the Fischel corporation (Costa Rican), Alcatel (French), and Instrumentarium (Finnish), as well as the Caja Costarricense de Seguro Social (Social Security) and the ICE. Important business leaders and politicians were arrested and imprisoned, among them the ex-presidents Calderón Fournier and Rodríguez. Another ex-President, Figueres Olsen has refused to return to the country to testify before the investigators overseeing the case.

In this context, and supported by the major part of the business sector and the principal media outlets, Arias declared himself strongly in favor of CAFTA. Meanwhile, President Abel Pacheco postponed sending CAFTA to the Legislative Assembly, which between the end of 2004 and the beginning of 2005 resulted in the resignation of the CAFTA negotiating team. The main media outlets responded to the president's approach with a systematic campaign to discredit his government – a government, it should be said, in which the fight against corruption was

I just want to note three that are now for many nothing but bureaucratic institutions: the National Insurance Institute (1924), Costa Rican Social Security (1941-43), and the Costa Rican Electricity Institute (1949). The Free Trade Agreement proposes modifying these so that they adapt to the new circumstances and to the old interests, according to the potent wishes of large international groups.

Eugenio Rodríguez, ex-Rector of the University of Costa Rica, September 2005.

Teachers and students against CAFTA, November 2005.

[O]*ut of respect for the memory of Rodrigo, my family and I have resolved to request that his name be immediately removed from the training institute of the Party of National Liberation. We don't want the name of Rodrigo Facio Brenes to continue being associated with an entity that no longer represents his ideals, or reflects his aspirations, or believes in his transformative thinking. Nor do we want his image to be linked to the party that used to defend the State of Welfare Rights and that today is an accomplice of those who malign it and seek its extermination...*

Leda Fernández, widow of Rodrigo Facio, May 2006.

intensified as never before in the history of Costa Rica.

The rapid erosion of the two-party system – an erosion that limited the margin of maneuverability for the neoliberals in the previous governments of Rodríguez and Pacheco – also favored the rise of new organizations. Among the more important are the Movimiento Libertario (Libertarian Movement), founded in 1994 as an ultra-neoliberal off-shoot of the PUSC, and the Citizens' Action Party (PAC), established in 2000 as a social-democratic off-shoot of the PLN. The results of the 2006 presidential elections were surprising: with a turnout of scarcely 65 percent, the PLN and the PUSC captured a scant 44 percent of the presidential and congressional vote, and Arias beat his principal rival, Ottón Solís of the PAC by a mere one percent of the valid votes cast.

With a fractious Legislative Assembly in which no party holds a majority and broad civil opposition to CAFTA, Costa Rican society will decide in the near future whether neoliberalism is entrenched or whether strategic social infrastructure shall remain under the state control. The decision will be made amidst commemorative celebrations of the sesquicentenary of the National Campaign, a war that saw Costa Ricans fighting to defend the existing social and institutional order of the country.

EPILOGUE

COSTA RICAN EXCEPTIONALISM

It would be wrong to end this brief history of Costa Rica on a note of uncertainty. On balance, the country's past is cause for optimism. Its people had a relatively miserable lot during the colonial era, and for most of the modern period they were dependent on one or two agricultural exports. Yet Costa Ricans were able to build political democracy and achieve a high degree of social justice in a region where dictatorship and grotesque inequalities have been the sad norm. Costa Rica is the only country in all of Latin America to have enjoyed consistent and uninterrupted democratic life since 1950. These are exceptional triumphs, and Costa Ricans are justifiably proud of them.

Costa Rica's success has been based on an extraordinary capacity to

Touring.

In the two years I spent in Costa Rica in the early 1980s... even in relatively remote communities in Guanacaste, I saw that dentists would come periodically to check people's teeth, that children received hot meals... that elderly or disabled people often received pensions, and that even many small producers or jornaleros *were insured by the Caja through relatives... I come, of course, from a society that has been severely, probably irreparably, damaged by twelve years of Reagan-Bush free-market madness very much like the model that has been imposed on Costa Rica since the mid-1980s... I... consider it useful to see Costa Rica as a significant experiment and a historical alternative in a world in which there is now... only one economic model, and one that has yet to prove its worth for the great majority.*

Marc Edelman, US anthropologist, 1993.

adapt processes of global change to its own local situation on the basis of gradual adjustments that have allowed the majority of the population to accommodate themselves slowly to new economic and institutional realities. Prior to 1950 the model chosen was agro-export growth with a social policy cushion, between 1950 and 1978 it was a mixed economy, and then from 1978 onwards it was trade liberalization with a large public sector. This permanent Costa Rican search for an alternative way confirms that Third World people make their own history, too, though they do not make it just as they choose.

Within the small spaces left to them in the grand design of the world economy and power politics, Costa Ricans were able to fashion an uncommonly democratic and equitable society. The present challenge is more intense than ever before, the room for maneuver extremely tight, but up to now Costa Ricans have found a way to give their peculiar Utopia new life in a world dominated by a globalizing capitalism. To the degree that they can maintain this achievement, new chapters on the history of Costa Rica will be necessary to explain the future of a society that discovered a very long time ago that the road that combines cultural development, democracy, and social justice is the only one worth following.

CHRONOLOGY

Year	Costa Rica	World
12,000-8,000 B.C.	Occupation of present-day Costa Rica by hunters and gatherers.	Paleolithic era.
8,000-4,000 B.C.	Initial settlements and accidental domestication of plants.	Neolithic era.
4,000-1,000 B.C.	Transition to the production of foodstuffs.	Bronze age; Ancient Egyptian empire.
1,000 B.C.-800 A.D.	Consolidation of agriculture.	Greek and Roman civilizations; early Middle Ages in Europe; Mayan empire in northern Central America and southern Mexico.
800-1500 A.D.	Development of chieftainships (*cacicazgos*), and growing social differentiation within indigenous societies.	Feudalism; Renaissance; European overseas expansion; Aztec empire in Valley of Mexico; Incan empire in Andes.
1492		Europeans discover America.
1502	Columbus lands in Cariay (present-day Limón).	

Year	Costa Rica	World
1510-1570	Conquest and demographic catastrophe of indigenous people.	Fall of Tenochtitlan (1521), and founding of Lima (1535).
1564	Founding of Cartago (the colonial capital) by Vázquez de Coronado.	
1569	Distribution of encomiendas by Perafán de Rivera.	
1570		Creation of Audiencia of Guatemala.
1590	Beginnings of mule trade.	
1620-1720		Crisis in Europe; decadence of Spain and economic ascent of England and Holland.
1635	Apparition of the Virgin of los Ángeles, according to the tradition.	
1650	Growth of leather and lard trade with Panama.	
1660	Expansion of cacao cultivation and import of black slaves.	
1702		Bourbon monarchy in Spain.
1706	Founding of Heredia.	
1709	Uprising of the Talamanca indigenous people.	
1710	Execution of the rebel leader, Pablo Presbere.	
1736	Founding of San José.	
1750	Opening of Guatemalan market to livestock of Pacific coast.	Expansion of indigo production in north of Central America; High Enlightenment and initial phase of industrialization in Western Europe.
1760	Expansion of tobacco cultivation.	Bourbon Reforms in Spain and Spanish America.
1766		Tobacco monopoly established in Audiencia of Guatemala.

Year	Costa Rica	World
1776		United States revolution for independence.
1781	Royal Tobacco Monopoly established in San José.	
1782	Founding of Alajuela.	
1789		French Revolution.
1808	Riots against tobacco monopoly.	Napoleonic invasion of Spain.
1810		Beginning of Independence movements in Spanish America (1810-24).
1812	Riots against liquor monopoly.	Constitution of Cadiz.
1814	Founding of the Casa de Enseñanza de Santo Tomás in San José.	
1820	Mining boom in the Montes del Aguacate (1820-43).	
1821	Independence of Central America (15 September).	Iturbide's Mexican Empire (1821-23).
1822	Free trade declared.	
1823	Battle of Ochomogo (5 April); San José becomes capital.	
1824	Annexation of Partido de Nicoya (25 July).	Founding of the Central American Federal Republic.
1830	Introduction of the printing press; importance of Brazil wood exports.	Francisco Morazán presides over Central American Federal Republic (1830-39).
1835	War of the League (October), won by San José.	
1838	Dictatorship of Carrillo (1838-42).	
1840	Boom in coffee exports begins.	Morazán defeated by Guatemalan rebels; end of the Central American Federal Republic.
1842	Morazán deposes Carrillo and becomes Head of State (April); overthrow and execution of Morazán (September).	

Year	Costa Rica	World
1843	Creation of University of Santo Tomás in San José.	
1848	Declaration of Republic of Costa Rica (30 August); new Constitution strips citizenship rights from thousands of Costa Ricans.	Marx and Engels publish the *Communist Manifesto*.
1849	Juan Rafael Mora takes power (1849-59).	Transport of passengers from east to west coast of the United States via the San Juan River.
1856	National Campaign against William Walker: Battle of Rivas (11 April 1856); cholera epidemic kills about 8 percent of populace (May-July); surrender of Walker (1 May 1857).	
1859	Fall of Juan Rafael Mora, executed in 1860; new Constitution establishes universal male suffrage in the first-round elections.	
1861		United States Civil War (1861-65).
1870	Dictatorship of Tomás Guardia (1870-82); beginning of construction of railroad to Caribbean coast (1870-90).	Second industrial wave in Europe and the United States; Paris Commune.
1871	Approval of the Constitution of 1871 (in force up to 1948, with the exception of 1876-82 and 1917-19).	
1877	Death penalty abolished (decree incorporated into the Constitution in 1882).	
1880	Beginning of Liberal reforms and banana exports; the cult of the Virgin of los Ángeles, promoted by the Church, begins to gain popularity outside of Cartago and to acquire a national character.	
1884	Expulsion of Bishop and religious orders; signing of Soto-Keith contract.	
1885	According to the electoral census, 63 percent of Costa Rican men 20 years old and over are registered to vote.	

Year	Costa Rica	World
1889	Popular uprising in defense of electoral victory of opposition candidate, José Joaquín Rodríguez (7 November); appearance of the first political parties.	
1890	Growing organization of urban artisans and workers.	
1891	Unveiling in Alajuela of statue of Juan Santamaría, hero of the Battle of Rivas.	
1895	Unveiling of National Monument.	
1896	Costa Rican monetary unit changes from peso to colón.	
1897	Inauguration of the National Theater with Gounod's Faust; beginning of construction of Pacific Railway (1897-1910); first movies in San José.	Collapse of coffee prices (1897-1907).
1899		Founding of United Fruit Company.
1900	Joaquín García Monge publishes *El moto* and *Hijas del campo*, the first Costa Rican novels.	
1902	End of the authoritarian government of Rafael Iglesias (1894-1902) and democratic opening; in the first decade of the 20th century the proportion of Costa Rican males registered to vote rises to 100 percent, the electoral turnout in 1905 and 1909 is greater than 72 percent and public spending in education, health and infrastructure rises.	
1903		United States sponsors independence of Panama.
1907	Charge that theory of evolution is being taught in Heredia secondary school begins the most important religious conflict in 20th-century Costa Rica.	
1910	Earthquake destroys Cartago; Halley's Comet causes panic.	Mexican Revolution begins (1910-20).
1913	Workers begin to celebrate May Day; introduction of the direct vote.	

Year	Costa Rica	World
1914	Reformist government of Alfredo González Flores (1914-17).	Opening of the Panama Canal; European War (1914-18).
1917	Tinoco dictatorship (1917-19).	Bolshevik Revolution in Russia.
1919	After fall of Tinoco dictatorship politics becomes more competitive and greater possibilities opened up for rural and urban popular classes to channel their demands via elections.	
1920	Successful strikes for the 8 hour day; influenza pandemic kills over 2,000.	
1923	Founding of Reformist Party and La Liga Feminista (12 October).	
1925-1927	Secret vote approved, women's vote rejected.	
1927	Creation of Ministry of Public Health.	Sandino's struggle against United States occupation of Nicaragua (1927-34).
1928	Creation of Ministry of Labor; beginning of plastic arts exhibitions (1928-37).	
1929	Panic in San José over consumption of heroin by workers.	Beginning of crisis of world capitalism.
1930	Beginning of economic crisis.	
1931	Founding of Communist Party.	
1932	Founding of National Association of Coffee Producers.	
1933	Founding of Institute for the Defence of Coffee.	
1934	Great strike of banana workers on Caribbean coast.	
1936	Banking reforms lay ground work for Banco Nacional and Superintendent of Banks.	Popular Front in France and Spain; Spanish Civil War (1936-39).
1939		Second World War (1939-45).

Year	Costa Rica	World
1940	Election of Rafael Ángel Calderón Guardia and beginning of social reform; founding of the Center for the Study of National Problems.	
1941	National Republican Party divides into Calderonistas and Cortesistas, beginning a cycle of polarization and political instability that will last until the late 1950s.	
1945	Beginning of post-war economic boom.	Beginning of the Cold War (1945-89).
1948	Civil War won by the Army of National Liberation, under leadership of José Figueres; persecution of Calderonistas and Communists.	
1949	Foundation of the Second Republic; Constitution of 1949 approved; black populace and women enfranchised.	Victory of the Chinese Communists.
1951	Founding of the political party, Liberación Nacional (PLN).	
1955	Failure of invasion of Costa Rica by forces backed by Nicaraguan dictator, Anastasio Somoza intending to overthrow José Figueres government.	
1959		Cuban revolution.
1960	Debut of television.	Treaty for Central American Integration.
1961		Kennedy announces Alliance for Progress, the "Marshall Plan" for Latin America.
1962	Public protest against electrical rate increases in Cartago is brutally repressed by the police at a cost of three deaths and 40 injured (23 November).	
1963	Costa Rica joins Central American Common Market; domination of Costa Rican industry by foreign capital.	
1964		Beginning of military intervention of United States in Vietnam war.

Year	Costa Rica	World
1968		Student-led revolts throughout the West; Prague spring.
1969	Presidential re-election prohibited.	The first men on the Moon.
1970	Student protests against concessions to the mining company, ALCOA (24 April).	
1972	Creation of CODESA.	Earthquake destroys Managua.
1973		Oil crisis.
1974	Daniel Oduber elected President; growth of entrepreneur state.	
1975	Reform of article 98 of the Constitution that had kept the Communist Party illegal since 1949.	
1978	Economic downturn.	
1979		Sandinista Revolution in Nicaragua.
1980	Explosion of economic crisis; growing traffic in arms and drugs.	Deepening of revolutionary wars in El Salvador and Guatemala; Ronald Reagan elected President of the USA (1980-88).
1982	Beginning of crisis of the left-wing parties.	
1983	Founding of the Party of Social Christian Unity (PUSC), and consolidation of two-party system; Costa Rica proclaims its neutrality; beginning of massive US aid so that Costa Rica will join the struggle against Communism in Central America.	Growing intervention of the US in Central American conflicts.
1984	Massive march for peace in San José; neoliberals gain ascendancy within PLN.	
1986	Founding of the National Center for the Development of Women and the Family, transformed into the National Women's Institute in 1998.	

Year	Costa Rica	World
1987	President Óscar Arias awarded Nobel Peace prize; boom in non-traditional export products, whose value exceeds the value of coffee and banana exports.	Signing of Central American Peace Plan.
1989	Sharp drop in international price of coffee (1989-93); creation of the Sala Cuarta (Constitutional chamber of the Supreme Court).	Fall of the Berlin Wall; end of Communist States in Eastern Europe; United States invades Panama.
1990	National Team wins two matches at World Cup and advances to second round; boom in tourist industry; government of Calderón Fournier begins "shock therapy"; at least 12 tons of cocaine enter the United States via Costa Rica.	Electoral defeat of Sandinistas in Nicaragua; deepening of peace process in El Salvador.
1991	Intensification of the neo-liberal adjustment; massive university protests against the funding cuts of Calderón Fournier government.	Pro-democracy movement crushed in Tiananmen Square, Beijing; collapse of Soviet Union; Gulf War.
1992	Creation of the ombudsman's office.	End of the Reagan-Bush era.
1994	Closing of Banco Anglo Costarricense (founded in 1863), due to massive corruption; the percentage of households living in poverty falls to roughly 20 percent and settles at that level.	Genocide in Rwanda.
1995	Political Pact between Figueres Olsen and Calderón Fournier, backed by the leadership of PLN and PUSC, to deepen neoliberal adjustment of economy; vast popular mobilizations against the Pact.	
1996	Acceleration of moves to privatize ICE; private banks begin to open current accounts (an option not available to them since 1948).	Second electoral defeat of Sandinismo in Nicaragua.
1997	INTEL begins operations; at least 50 tons of cocaine enter the United States via Costa Rica; political parties obliged to fill a minimum of 40 percent of their eligible posts with women.	
1998	Electoral turnout in presidential elections falls to 70 percent.	

Year	Costa Rica	World
2000		Controversial and questionable election of George W. Bush to presidency of US.
2001	Massive popular mobilizations in March and April against the project to privatize ICE and other public institutions.	Attack against the twin towers in New York (11 September); US invades Afghanistan.
2002	Crisis in two-party system deepens; for the first time, a second round of presidential elections is necessary after no candidate gets more than 40 percent of the vote (the necessary threshold for winning the presidency).	
2003	Central America and US negotiate free trade agreement; Constitutional Court overturns the prohibition on presidential re-election.	Worldwide repudiation of the invasion of Iraq by US and Great Britain.
2004	Ex-presidents Rafael Ángel Calderón Fournier and Miguel Ángel Rodríguez jailed on corruption charges; ex-President José María Figueres Olsen declines to return to Costa Rica to answer questions about payments received from the transnational company, Alcatel; President Abel Pacheco postpones sending the Central American Free Trade Agreement (CAFTA) to the Legislative Assembly; principal media outlets begin systematic campaign to tarnish the image of the Pacheco government.	Tsunami kills more than 230,000 people around the Indian Ocean; China is the fifth largest economy of the world; eight countries of Eastern Europe enter European Union.
2005	New immigration law criminalizes all those involved in illegal immigrant trafficking.	Bombs in Madrid and London transport systems.
2006	Óscar Arias wins the presidency by a narrow margin; Costa Rica commemorates 150th anniversary of the defeat of William Walker in a context dominated by popular mobilizations against the Central American Free Trade Agreement (CAFTA).	United States militarizes border with Mexico; civil war in US-occupied Iraq.

BIBLIOGRAPHY

General

Bulmer-Thomas, Victor, *The Political Economy of Central America since 1920*. Cambridge: Cambridge University Press, 1987.

Edelman, Marc, and Joanne Kenen, eds., *The Costa Rica Reader*. New York: Grove Weidenfeld, 1989.

Palmer, Steven, and Iván Molina, eds., *The Costa Rica Reader: History, Culture, Politics*. Durham and London: Duke University Press, 2004.

Pérez, Héctor, *Breve historia contemporánea de Costa Rica*. México: Fondo de Cultura Económica, 1997.

Pérez, Héctor, *A Brief History of Central America*. Berkeley: University of California Press, 1989.

Torres-Rivas, Edelberto, et al., *Historia general de Centroamérica*, 6 vols. Madrid: FLACSO-Quinto Centenario, 1993.

Woodward, Ralph Lee, Jr., *Central America: A Nation Divided*, 3d ed. New York: Oxford University Press, 1999.

Web Sites

http://nacion.com/
La Nación, Costa Rica's most important daily newspaper, with numerous links, a free archive, and an English-language edition.
http://www.ticotimes.net/
Costa Rica's good English-language weekly paper.

http://www.semanario.ucr.ac.cr/
University of Costa Rica weekly, the most independent newspaper in the country.
http://www.casapres.go.cr/
The President of Costa Rica, with links to most government ministries and autonomous state agencies.
http://www.tse.go.cr/
The Supreme Electoral Tribunal, with electoral results and other political data from the 1950s onward.
http://www.inec.go.cr/
National Institute of Statistics and Census of Costa Rica, with free access to important economic, social, and demographic data.
http://www.metabase.net/
METABASE, a site integrating many Central American libraries and library catalogues.
http://historia.fcs.ucr.ac.cr/
The School of History at the University of Costa Rica, with two electronic publications, *Diálogos: Revista Electrónica de Historia* and *Cuadernos Digitales*, and links to other historical and social science research institutes.
http://ccp.ucr.ac.cr/
The Central American Population Center of the University of Costa Rica, with important documents and data bases on Central American and especially Costa Rican demographics.
http://www.estadonacion.or.cr/
The Estado de la Nación (state of the nation) project, updated year by year to provide an analysis of Costa Rica's economic, social, political, cultural, environmental, and gender situation.
http://www.flacso.or.cr/
Information on the work and publications of FLACSO-Costa Rica, the most important independent academic program of the country.

Ancient and Colonial Periods

Corrales, Francisco, *Los primeros costarricenses*. San José: Museo Nacional, 2001.

Fonseca, Elizabeth, Patricia Alvarenga, and Juan Carlos Solórzano, *Costa Rica en el siglo XVIII*. San José: Editorial de la Universidad de Costa Rica, 2001.

Fonseca, Óscar, *Historia antigua de Costa Rica: surgimiento y caracterización de la primera civilización costarricense*. San José: Editorial de la Universidad de Costa Rica, 1992.

Ibarra, Eugenia, *Las sociedades cacicales de Costa Rica (siglo XVI)*. San José: Editorial de la Universidad de Costa Rica, 1990.

Quirós, Claudia, *La era de la encomienda*. San José: Editorial de la Universidad de Costa Rica, 1990.

Colonial Legacy and Coffee Expansion

Acuña, Víctor Hugo, and Iván Molina, *Historia económica y social de Costa Rica (1750-1950)*. San José: Editorial Porvenir, 1991.

Gudmundson, Lowell, *Costa Rica Before Coffee: Society and Economy on the Eve of the Export Boom*. Baton Rouge: Louisiana State University Press, 1986.

Hall, Carolyn, *El café y el desarrollo histórico geográfico de Costa Rica*, 3d ed. San José: Editorial Costa Rica, 1982.

León, Jorge, *Evolución del comercio exterior y del transporte marítimo de Costa Rica 1821-1900*. San José: Editorial de la Universidad de Costa Rica, 1997.

Molina, Iván, *Costa Rica (1800-1850). El legado colonial y la génesis del capitalismo*. San José: Editorial de la Universidad de Costa Rica, 1991.

Samper, Mario, "Generations of Settlers: A Study of Rural Households and their Markets on the Costa Rican Frontier, 1850-1935". Ph. D., University of California, 1987 (Westview Press published one version of this work in 1990).

Politics and Democracy before 1950

Acuña, Víctor Hugo, *Conflicto y reforma en Costa Rica: 1940-1949*. San José: Editorial Universidad Estatal a Distancia, 1991.

Lehoucq, Fabrice, "The Origins of Democracy in Costa Rica in Comparative Perspective". Ph. D., Duke University, 1992.

Lehoucq, Fabrice, and Iván Molina, *Stuffing the Ballot Box. Fraud, Electoral Reform, and Democratization in Costa Rica*. New York: Cambridge University Press, 2002.

Miller, Eugene D., *A Holy Alliance? The Church and the Left in Costa Rica, 1932-1948*. Armonk: M. E. Sharpe, 1996.

Molina, Iván, *Demoperfectocracia. La democracia pre-reformada en Costa Rica (1885-1948)*. Heredia: Editorial Universidad Nacional, 2005.

Muñoz, Mercedes, *El Estado y la abolición del ejército en Costa Rica, 1914-1949*. San José: Editorial Porvenir, 1990.

Salazar, Jorge Mario, *Crisis liberal y Estado reformista. Análisis político electoral, 1914-1949*. San José: Editorial de la Universidad de Costa Rica, 1995.

Salazar, Orlando, *El apogeo de la república liberal en Costa Rica, 1870-1914*. San José: Editorial de la Universidad de Costa Rica, 1990.

Soto, Gustavo Adolfo, *La Iglesia costarricense y la cuestión social.* San José: Editorial Universidad Estatal a Distancia, 1985.

Vargas, Claudio, *El liberalismo, la Iglesia y el Estado en Costa Rica.* San José: Alma Máter and Guayacán, 1991.

Vargas, Hugo, *El sistema electoral en Costa Rica durante el siglo XIX.* San José: Editorial de la Universidad de Costa Rica, 2005.

Social and Cultural History from 1750 to 1950

Fumero, Patricia, *Teatro, público y Estado en San José (1880-1914).* San José: Editorial de la Universidad de Costa Rica, 1996.

Gil, José Daniel, *El culto a la Virgen de los Ángeles (1824-1935). Una aproximación a la mentalidad religiosa en Costa Rica.* Alajuela: Museo Histórico Cultural Juan Santamaría, 2004.

Molina, Iván, and Steven Palmer, eds., *El paso del cometa. Estado, política social y culturas populares en Costa Rica (1800-1950),* 2d ed. San José: Editorial Universidad Estatal a Distancia, 2005.

Molina, Iván, and Steven Palmer, eds., *Héroes al gusto y libros de moda. Sociedad y cambio cultural en Costa Rica (1750-1900),* 2d ed. San José: Editorial Universidad Estatal a Distancia, 2004.

Morales, Gerardo, *Cultura oligárquica y nueva intelectualidad en Costa Rica: 1880-1914.* Heredia: Editorial Universidad Nacional, 1993.

Moya, Arnaldo, *Comerciantes y damas principales de Cartago: vida cotidiana (1750-1820).* Cartago: Editorial Cultural Cartaginesa, 1998.

Murillo, Carmen, *Identidades de hierro y humo. La construcción del Ferrocarril al Atlántico 1870-1890.* San José: Editorial Porvenir, 1995.

Oliva, Mario, *Artesanos y obreros costarricenses, 1880-1914.* San José: Editorial Costa Rica, 1985.

Quesada, Florencia, *En el barrio Amón. Arquitectura, familia y sociabilidad del primer residencial de la elite urbana de San José, 1900-1935.* San José: Editorial de la Universidad de Costa Rica, 2001.

Urbina, Chester, *Costa Rica y el deporte (1873-1921). Un estudio acerca del origen del fútbol y la construcción de un deporte nacional.* Heredia: Editorial Universidad Nacional, 2001.

Vargas, María Clara, *De las fanfarrias a las salas de concierto. Música en Costa Rica (1840-1940).* San José: Editorial de la Universidad de Costa Rica, 2004.

Vega, Patricia, *De la imprenta al periódico. Los inicios de la comunicación impresa en Costa Rica 1821-1850.* San José: Editorial Porvenir, 1995.

Social Policy before 1950

Malavassi, Ana Paulina, *Entre la marginalidad social y los orígenes de la salud pública: leprosos, curanderos y facultativos en el Valle Central de Costa Rica (1784-1845)*. San José: Editorial de la Universidad de Costa Rica, 2003.

Molina, Iván, *La aclimatación imposible. Cuestión social y anticomunismo en Costa Rica (1931-1948)*. San José: Editorial Costa Rica, 2007.

Molina, Iván, and Steven Palmer, *Educando a Costa Rica. Alfabetización popular, formación docente y género (1880-1950)*, 2d ed. San José: Editorial Universidad Estatal a Distancia, 2003.

Palmer, Steven, *From Popular Medicine to Medical Populism. Doctors, Healers, and Public Power in Costa Rica, 1800-1940*. Durham: Duke University Press, 2003.

Viales, Ronny, ed., *Pobreza e historia en Costa Rica. Determinantes estructurales y representaciones sociales del siglo XVIII a 1950*. San José: Editorial de la Universidad de Costa Rica, 2005.

Gender and Women's History

González, Alfonso, *Vida cotidiana en la Costa Rica del siglo XIX: un estudio psicogenético*. San José: Editorial de la Universidad de Costa Rica, 1997.

Mora, Virginia, *Rompiendo mitos y forjando historia. Mujeres urbanas y relaciones de género en Costa Rica a inicios del siglo XX*. Alajuela: Museo Histórico Cultural Juan Santamaría, 2003.

Rodríguez, Eugenia, *Divorcio y violencia de pareja en Costa Rica (1800-1950)*. Heredia: Editorial Universidad Nacional, 2006.

Rodríguez, Eugenia, ed., *Mujeres, género e historia en América Central durante los siglos XVIII, XIX y XX*. San José: UNIFEM and Plumsock Mesoamerican Studies, 2002.

Rodríguez, Eugenia, *Hijas novias y esposas. Familia, matrimonio y violencia doméstica en el Valle Central de Costa Rica (1750-1850)*. Heredia: Editorial Universidad Nacional, 2000.

Rodríguez, Eugenia, ed., *Entre silencios y voces. Género e historia en América Central (1750-1990)*. San José: Editorial Porvenir y Centro Nacional para el Desarrollo de la Mujer y la Familia, 1997.

Sandoval, Carlos, *Fuera de juego. Fútbol, identidades nacionales y masculinidades*. San José: Editorial de la Universidad de Costa Rica, 2006.

Schifter, Jacobo, and Johnny Madrigal, *Las gavetas sexuales del costarricense y el riesgo de infección con el VIH*. San José: Imediex, 1996.

The Nation and Nationalism

Díaz, David, "La fiesta de la independencia en Costa Rica, 1821-1921". Tesis de Maestría en Historia, Universidad de Costa Rica, 2001.

Hayden, Bridget A., *Salvadorans in Costa Rica. Displaced Lives.* Tucson: University of Arizona Press, 2003.

Molina, Iván, *Costarricense por dicha. Identidad nacional y cambio cultural en Costa Rica durante los siglos XIX y XX.* San José: Editorial de la Universidad de Costa Rica, 2002.

Molina, Iván, and Francisco Enríquez, eds., *Fin de siglo XIX e identidad nacional en México y Centroamérica.* Alajuela: Museo Histórico Cultural Juan Santamaría, 2000.

Pakkasvirta, Jussi, *¿Un continente, una nación? Intelectuales latinoamericanos, comunidad política y las revistas culturales en Costa Rica y en el Perú (1919-1930).* Helsinki: Academia Scientiarum Fennica, 1997.

Palmer, Steven, "A Liberal Discipline: Inventing Nations in Guatemala and Costa Rica 1870-1900". Ph. D., Columbia University, 1990.

Sandoval, Carlos, *Threatening Others: Nicaraguans and the Formation of National Identities in Costa Rica.* Athens: Ohio University Press, 2004.

Soto, Ronald, "Inmigración e identidad nacional en Costa Rica. 1904-1942. Los 'otros' reafirman el 'nosotros'". Tesis de Licenciatura en Historia, Universidad de Costa Rica, 1998.

Taracena, Arturo, and Jean Piel, eds., *Identidades nacionales y Estado moderno en Centroamérica.* San José: Editorial de la Universidad de Costa Rica, 1995.

Art and Literature

Mosby, Dorothy E., *Place, Language and Identity in Afro-Costa Rican Literature.* Columbia: University of Missouri Press, 2003.

Quesada, Álvaro, *Breve historia de la literatura costarricense.* San José: Editorial Porvenir, 2000.

Quesada, Álvaro, *Uno y los otros. Identidad y literatura en Costa Rica 1890-1940.* San José: Editorial de la Universidad de Costa Rica, 1998.

Rojas, Margarita, and Flora Ovares, *100 años de literatura costarricense.* San José: Farben-Norma, 1995.

Sharman, Russell, "With the Vision They See: Identity and Aesthetic Experience in Puerto Limón, Costa Rica". Ph. D., Oxford University, 1999.

Zavaleta, Eugenia, *Las exposiciones de artes plásticas en Costa Rica (1928-1937).* San José: Editorial de la Universidad de Costa Rica, 2004.

Zavaleta, Eugenia, *Los inicios del arte abstracto en Costa Rica 1958-1971.* San José: Museo de Arte Costarricense, 1994.

Regional History

Bourgois, Philippe, *Ethnicity at Work: Divided Labor on a Central American Banana Plantation.* Baltimore: The Johns Hopkins University Press, 1989.

Buska, Soili, "'Marimba por tí me muero'. Region and Nation in Costa Rica, 1824-1939". Ph. D., Indiana University, 2006.

Chomsky, Aviva, *West Indian Workers and the United Fruit Company in Costa Rica, 1870-1940*. Baton Rouge: Louisiana State University Press, 1996.

Edelman, Marc, *The Logic of the Latifundio: The Large Estates of Northwestern Costa Rica Since the Late Nineteenth Century*. Stanford: Stanford University Press, 1992.

Harpelle, Ronald N., *The West Indian Workers and the United Fruit Company in Costa Rica since the Late Nineteenth Century*. Montreal: McGill-Queens University Press, 2001.

Palmer, Paula, *"What Happen": A Folk History of Costa Rica's Talamanca Coast*. San José: Editorama, 1993.

Putnam, Lara, *The Company They Kept: Migrants and the Politics of Gender in Caribbean Costa Rica 1870-1960*. Chapel Hill: University of North Carolina Press, 2002.

Viales, Ronny, *Después del enclave 1927-1950: un estudio de la región atlántica costarricense*. San José: Editorial de la Universidad de Costa Rica and Museo Nacional, 1998.

From 1950 to the Present

Alvarenga, Patricia, *De vecinos a ciudadanos. Movimientos comunales y luchas cívicas en la historia contemporánea de Costa Rica*. San José: Editorial de la Universidad de Costa Rica-Editorial Universidad Nacional, 2005.

Bowman, Kirk, *Militarization, Democracy, and Development: The Perils of Praetorianism in Latin America*. University Park: The Pennsylvania State University Press, 2002.

Clark, Mary A., *Gradual Economic Reform in Latin America: The Costa Rica Experience*. Albany: State University of New York Press, 2001.

Cuevas, Rafael, *El punto sobre la i. Políticas culturales en Costa Rica (1948-1990)*. San José: Ministerio de Cultura, Juventud y Deportes, 1995.

Edelman, Marc, *Peasants against Globalization: Rural Social Movements in Costa Rica*. Stanford: Stanford University Press, 1999.

González, Alfonso, *Mujeres y hombres de la posguerra costarricense (1950-1960)*. San José: Editorial de la Universidad de Costa Rica, 2005.

González, Alfonso, and Manuel Solís, *Entre el desarraigo y el despojo… Costa Rica en el fin de siglo*. San José: Editorial de la Universidad de Costa Rica, 2001.

Hall, Carolyn, *Costa Rica: A Geographical Interpretation in Historical Perspective*. Boulder, Colorado: Westview Press, 1985.

Lehoucq, Fabrice, *Lucha electoral y sistema político en Costa Rica 1948-1998*. San José: Editorial Porvenir, 1997.

Mesa-Lago, Carmelo, et al., *Market, Socialist, and Mixed Economies: Comparative Policy and Performance: Chile, Cuba, and Costa Rica*. Baltimore: Johns Hopkins University Press, 2000.

Opazo, Andrés, *Costa Rica: la Iglesia católica y el orden social*. San José: Departamento Ecuménico de Investigaciones, 1987.

Programa Estado de la Nación, *Estado de la nación en desarrollo humano sostenible*, 1-11. San José: Programa Estado de la Nación, 1994-2005.

Raventós, Ciska, et al., *Abstencionistas en Costa Rica. ¿Quiénes son y por qué no votan?* San José: Editorial de la Universidad de Costa Rica, 2005.

Rodríguez, Carlos, *Tierra de labriegos. Los campesinos en Costa Rica desde 1950*. San José: FLACSO, 1993.

Rosero, Luis, ed., *Costa Rica a la luz del Censo del 2000*. San José: Centro Centroamericano de Población, 2004.

Rovira, Jorge, ed., *La democracia de Costa Rica ante el siglo XXI*. San José: Editorial de la Universidad de Costa Rica, 2001.

Rovira, Jorge, *Costa Rica en los años '80*. San José: Editorial Porvenir, 1987.

Rovira, Jorge, *Estado y política económica en Costa Rica, 1948-1970*. San José: Editorial Porvenir, 1982.

Sandoval, Carlos, *Sueños y sudores en la vida cotidiana. Trabajadores y trabajadoras de la maquila y la construcción en Costa Rica*. San José: Editorial de la Universidad de Costa Rica, 1997.

Wilson, Bruce M., *Costa Rica: Politics, Economics, and Democracy*. Boulder: Lynne Rienner, 1998.

ILLUSTRATIONS

Travelers. Fernández Guardia, Ricardo, comp., *Costa Rica en el siglo XIX. Antología de viajeros*, 4th ed. (San José: Editorial Universitaria Centroamericana, 1982). p. 10 ix

Arrowheads, Turrialba, 12,000-8,000 B.C. Fonseca, Óscar, *Historia antigua de Costa Rica: surgimiento y caracterización de la primera civilización costarricense* (San José: Editorial de la Universidad de Costa Rica, 1992), p. 77 1

Scraping instruments, Turrialba, 12,000-8,000 B.C. Fonseca, *Historia antigua*, p. 77 2

Hunting turtles. "Álbum de Figueroa", Archivo Nacional de Costa Rica 3

Figure on a *metate* (used for preparing food), Pacific north, 500-800 A.D. Museo Nacional de Costa Rica 4

Figure of a shaman, Atlantic area, 500-1000 A.D. Museo Nacional de Costa Rica 5

Indigenous vessel. "Álbum de Figueroa" 6

Area of Chibcha influence, c. 800 A.D. Fonseca, *Historia antigua*, p. 40 7

Stone sphere in the Nacional Museum, Pacific south, 1-500 A.D. Museo Nacional de Costa Rica 8

Indigenous community. "Álbum de Figueroa" 9

Warrior with axe and head, Atlantic area, 500-1000 A.D. Museo Nacional de Costa Rica 10

Indigenous people in the forest. "Álbum de Figueroa"   11
Cacicazgos and *señoríos* of Costa Rica, 16th century. Ibarra, Euge-
    nia, *Las sociedades cacicales de Costa Rica (siglo XVI)* (San
    José: Editorial de la Universidad de Costa Rica, 1990), p. 28   13
Sacred struggle between light and darkness (detail), Pacific north,
    800-1350 A.D. Museo Nacional de Costa Rica   14
Indigenous Dwelling in Sipurio, Talamanca. Oil on canvas. Luis San-
    clemente, 1892. Museo Nacional de Costa Rica   15
The end of one civilization and the beginning of another. "Álbum de
    Figueroa"   18
Indigenous resistance. "Álbum de Figueroa"   19
Audiencia of Guatemala, c. 1800. Hall, Carolyn, *El café y el desar-
    rollo histórico geográfico de Costa Rica*, 3d ed. (San José: Edi-
    torial Costa Rica, 1982), p. 26   21
Exploration of Costa Rican Pacific coast. "Álbum de Figueroa"   22
Whipping and dismemberment of indigenous people. "Álbum de
    Figueroa"   24
Spanish settlements, 16th century. Quirós, Claudia, *La era de la en-
    comienda* (San José: Editorial de la Universidad de Costa Rica,
    1990), p. 69   25
Exploitation of indigenous people. "Álbum de Figueroa"   26
Bows and arrows against firearms. "Álbum de Figueroa"   27
Commerce. "Álbum de Figueroa"   29
Exporting mules. "Álbum de Figueroa"   31
The Costa Rican economy of the 16th and 17th centuries. Quirós, *La
    era de la encomienda*, p. 286   32
The road to Matina. "Álbum de Figueroa"   33
The execution of Presbere in 1710. "Álbum de Figueroa"   36
The beginnings of San José. "Álbum de Figueroa"   37
Grinding rice or coffee by hand. Fernández Guardia, *Costa Rica en
    el siglo XIX*, cover picture   39
Market day in Cartago. Fernández Guardia, *Costa Rica en el siglo
    XIX*, p. 500   41
A peasant. Fernández Guardia, *Costa Rica en el siglo XIX*, p. 422   42
Trapiche (sugar mill). Fernández Guardia, *Costa Rica en el siglo
    XIX*, p. 255   44
Settlements, ports and roads of Costa Rica, 1750-1821. Molina, Iván,
    *Costa Rica (1800-1850). El legado colonial y la génesis del
    capitalismo* (San José: Editorial de la Universidad de Costa
    Rica, 1991), p. 83   46
Economic zones of Costa Rica, 1750-1821. Molina, *Costa Rica
    (1800-1850)*, p. 20   47
Holy Week in San José, 1858. Fernández Guardia, *Costa Rica en el
    siglo XIX*, p. 390   48

El Laberinto (The Labyrinth), a coffee estate near San José. Fernández Guardia, *Costa Rica en el siglo XIX*, p. 73   50

The *cabildo* of Cartago. "Álbum de Figueroa"   53

Principal barracks of San José, 1858. Fernández Guardia, *Costa Rica en el siglo XIX*, p. 465   54

Cathedral of San José, 1858. Fernández Guardia, *Costa Rica en el siglo XIX*, p. 287   56

Morazán disembarks in Costa Rica, 1842. "Álbum de Figueroa"   57

Cockfight in San José, 1858. Fernández Guardia, *Costa Rica en el siglo XIX*, p. 186   60

Teatro Nacional, San José, 1909. Zamora, Fernando, *Álbum de vistas de Costa Rica* (San José: no publisher, 1909), photo 9   61

The *Zapatería Francesa*, a shoeshop in San José, 1858. Fernández Guardia, *Costa Rica en el siglo XIX*, p. 378   62

Picking coffee in Tres Ríos, Cartago, 1920. Archivo Nacional de Costa Rica   63

Settlement of the western Central Valley, 1782-1866. Samper, Mario, "Generations of Settlers: A Study of Rural Households and their Markets on the Costa Rican Frontier, 1850-1935" (Ph.D., University of California, 1987), p. 150b   64

Carretas (ox carts). Fernández Guardia, *Costa Rica en el siglo XIX*, p. 8   65

Juan Rafael Mora Porras. Oil on canvas. Tomás Povedano, 1925. Museo Histórico Cultural Juan Santamaría, Alajuela   66

The Burning of the Mesón. Oil on canvas. Enrique Echandi, 1896. Museo Histórico Cultural Juan Santamaría, Alajuela   67

Tomás Guardia Gutiérrez. Oil on canvas. A. Esttagny, no date. Museo Histórico Cultural Juan Santamaría, Alajuela   69

Public school in Liberia, Guanacaste, 1909. Zamora, Álbum de vistas, photo 88   71

Independence Day, c. 1895. *Revista de Costa Rica en el siglo XIX*, t. I (San José: Tipografía Nacional, 1901), p. 175   72

Procession of the Virgin of los Ángeles, c. 1926. Archivo Nacional de Costa Rica   73

Barracks of Alajuela, 1909. Zamora, *Álbum de vistas*, photo 66   75

The chamber of the old Costa Rican Congress, 1909. Zamora, *Álbum de vistas*, photo 19   76

The railroad in the Central Valley, c. 1873. Archivo Nacional de Costa Rica   77

Loading bananas, 1909. Zamora, *Álbum de vistas*, photo 78   79

Sugar mill in Juan Viñas, Cartago, 1922. Gómez Miralles, Manuel, *Costa Rica, América Central*, 1922 (San José: no publisher, 1922), p. 188   81

Corral at El Viejo, Guanacaste, 1909. Zamora, *Álbum de vistas*, photo 87   82

Gold mine in Abangares, Guanacaste, 1922. Gómez Miralles, *Costa Rica, América Central*, p. 199 83

The Society of Artisans of Costa Rica, c. 1924. Archivo Nacional de Costa Rica 85

Cleto González Víquez on the campaign trail, c. 1927. Salazar, Jorge Mario, *Crisis liberal y Estado reformista. Análisis político electoral, 1914-1949* (San José: Editorial de la Universidad de Costa Rica, 1995), p. 132 86

Joaquín García Monge and his wife, Celia Carrillo, c. 1909. García Monge, Joaquín, *Obras escogidas* (San José: Editorial Universitaria Centroamericana, 1974), p. 305 88

Large shoeshop, 1909. Zamora, *Álbum de vistas*, photo 39 89

Solón Núñez, promoter of the public health, 1910. *Páginas Ilustradas*, 1 January 1910, p. 111 90

Maternity. Sculpture in stone. Francisco Zúñiga, 1935. Museo de Arte Costarricense 93

Women's Vote – the Day That They Get It. Newspaper cartoon. Paco Hernández, July 1923. Hernández, Paco, *Caricaturas en el Diario de Costa Rica, San José 1922-1924* (San José: Imprenta Alsina, 1924), p. 93 94

Librería Española bookstore, 1922. Gómez Miralles, *Costa Rica, América Central*, p. 45 95

The Paperboy. Oil on canvas. Rigoberto Moya, 1929. Patronato Nacional de la Infancia 96

Cleto González Víquez (1906) and Ricardo Jiménez Oreamuno (c. 1910), Costa Rica's "Olympian princes". *Páginas Ilustradas*, 8 May 1906, p. 1485 and Archivo Nacional de Costa Rica 98

Workers pick coffee near San José, 1922. Gómez Miralles, *Costa Rica, América Central*, p. 171 99

Adobe House. Oil on canvas. Fausto Pacheco, no date. Collection of Julio Jiménez 101

The Communist Party celebrates the publication of *Mamita Yunai*, July 1941. *Trabajo*, 26 July 1941, p. 1 102

"Buy *Trabajo*" (the Communist weekly), October 1938. *Trabajo*, 8 October 1938, p. 2 103

The celebration of the 300th anniversary of the Virgin of los Ángeles was dominated by anti-Communism, 1935. Borge C. Carlos, ed., *Tricentenario de Nuestra Señora de los Ángeles patrona oficial de Costa Rica 1635-1935* (San José: Imprenta Lehmann, 1941), between pages 576-577 104

Manuel Mora, Monseñor Sanabria and Calderón Guardia, 1943. Archivo Nacional de Costa Rica 106

Opposition march of women calling for electoral guarantees, August 1947. Museo Nacional de Costa Rica 109

Otilio Ulate campaigning in San Ignacio de Acosta, San José province, January 1948. Salazar, *Crisis liberal y Estado reformista*, p. 261 — 110

Carlos Monge Alfaro in 1972. *Universidad*, 3 July 1972, p. 3 — 112

The Tragedy of Costa Rica, memoirs of a Calderonista exile, 1951. Albertazzi, José, *La tragedia de Costa Rica* (Mexico: no publisher, 1951), cover picture — 114

Figueres during the act that abolished the army, 1948. Museo Nacional de Costa Rica — 115

Rector of the University of Costa Rica, Rodrigo Facio, lunches with faculty and students in the 1950s. Archivo de la Universidad de Costa Rica — 117

Figueres in the Victory Parade, 1948. Archivo Nacional de Costa Rica — 118

First day of classes at the University of Costa Rica, March 1971. *Universidad*, 8 March 1971, p. 8 — 119

Processing lard at the Numar plant (then a subsidiary of the United Fruit Company), c. 1960s. Archivo Nacional de Costa Rica — 121

Workers at the Costa Rican Tobacco Company, c. 1950s. Archivo Nacional de Costa Rica — 122

Figueres and Monseñor Odio at the official opening of the Tibás electric plant, San José province, 1956. Archivo Nacional de Costa Rica — 123

José Figueres transfers power to Daniel Oduber, 8 May 1974. Collection of *Universidad* — 124

Calderón Guardia and his son, Rafael Ángel Calderón Fournier, return to Costa Rica, 1958. Archivo Nacional de Costa Rica — 127

Juan Rafael Morales, 1999. Collection of Juan Rafael Morales — 129

Cover of *Our Voice*. *Nuestra Voz*, San José, February 1967, p. 1 — 131

The Gorillas, a poster in support of a banana workers's strike, by the Student Federation of the University of Costa Rica, c. 1971. Collection of Carlos Manuel Molina Jiménez — 132

Public transportation between the cities of San José and Alajuela, c. 1950s. Centro Alajuelense de la Cultura — 135

Schiller's *María Estuardo* at the University Theater, September 1975. *Universidad*, 1 September 1975, p. 6 — 136

The 24th of April 1970 in San José. Comisión Costarricense Pro-Democracia y Libertad, *Una jornada patriótica. 24 de abril de 1970* (no place, no publisher, no date), no page number — 139

Machinery in the Saprissa Textile Factory, San José, September 1977. *Universidad*, 2 September 1977, p. 3 — 141

Long Live Independence. Newspaper cartoon. Hugo Díaz, September 1972. *Universidad*, 11 September 1972, p. 4 — 142

President Rodrigo Carazo and his wife, Estrella Zeledón, in Sandinista Nicaragua, August 1980. *Universidad*, 29 August 1980, p. 25 — 144

Workers protest in San José, c. 1981. *Universidad*, 30 April 1982, p. 1   145

Ronald Reagan and Luis Alberto Monge at the White House, November 1982. Collection of *Universidad*   147

Peace march in San José, 15 May 1984. *Universidad*, 18 May 1984, p. 1   150

Peasants and farmers opine about the economic policies of the Arias government, San José, September 1986. Archivo Nacional de Costa Rica   152

March demanding government funding for public universities, October 1986. Collection of *Universidad*   154

March against the reform of the pension laws, August 1995. *Universidad*, 11 August 1995, p. 1   156

"The ICE is not for sale", March 2000. Collection of *Universidad*   157

President Oduber on a pineapple farm, c. 1976. Archivo Nacional de Costa Rica   158

A work day at INTEL, c. 2000. Collection of *Universidad*   159

An earlier style of promoting tourism in Costa Rica, 1938. Government of Costa Rica, *Cuatro años de la administración Cortés 1936-1940* (San José: Tipografía Nacional, 1940), no page number   160

The San Pedro Mall under construction in San José, November 1993. Collection of *Universidad*   162

Maquiladora workers, c. 1980s. Collection of *Universidad*   164

Teatro Chic (movie theater) in Alajuela, c. 1960s, today part of a bank. Centro Alajuelense de la Cultura   168

Holy Week, March 1985. Collection of *Universidad*   170

Banana workers, December 1992. Collection of *Universidad*   171

Old age and poverty, c. 2005. Collection of *Universidad*   174

Protest march of employees against the closing of the Banco Anglo Costarricense, 13 September 1994. *Universidad*, 16 September 1994, p. 1   176

Employers give their workers time off to rally for CAFTA, October 2005. Collection of *Universidad*   178

Teachers and students against CAFTA, November 2005. Collection of *Universidad*   179

Touring. Fernández Guardia, *Costa Rica en el siglo XIX*, p. 19   181

INDEX

A Ras del Suelo, 137
Acuña, Ángela, 93
Adobe House, 101
Afro-Caribbeans, 79-80, 90, 116, 137; assimilation of, 137; *see also*: ethnicity, racism
agriculture, 2-5, 9, 12, 38-43, 46, 49, 51, 69, 80, 128-129, 143, 161-163; African palm, 120; beans, 3, 29, 34, 38, 149; colonization, 63, 65-66, 83, 137-138; corn, 2-4, 12, 17, 29-30, 34, 38; diversification, 81-82, 120-121, 141; frontier, 39, 51, 63, 134, 151; pineapple, 158; rice, 39, 120; *see also*: bananas, cacao, coffee, sugar, tobacco
Alajuela, 14, 38-40, 45, 52-54, 63-64, 68, 75, 78, 104, 107, 135, 168; Naranjo, 133; Poás, 31; San Carlos, 13, 27, 45, 64; San Ramón, 64, 161; Turrúcares, 65
Alcatel, 179
ALCOA, 139, 165
Alliance of Costa Rican Women, 130-131
Amazon region, 161
America, 1
Amighetti, Francisco, 137
anarchism, 88, 91
anti-Communism, 103-105, 107, 128, 138, 177

anti-imperialism, 80
Antilles, 20
architecture, 48, 59-60, 95, 101, 123
Arévalo, Juan José, 113
Arias Sánchez, Óscar, 149, 151-153, 166, 178-180; Nobel Peace Prize, 152-153
Army of National Liberation, 114
Arrieta Villalobos, Román, 155
artisans, x, 29-30, 40, 42-43, 48, 62, 55, 67, 70, 75, 84-86, 88, 91, 96-97, 129, 132; exploitation of, 42-43; *see also*: crafts, workers
artists, 87, 96, 137; *see also*: plastic arts
Asia, 1
Atlantic area, 5, 10; *see also*: Caribbean
Atlantic Railway, 64, 77-79; *see also*: railroads
Auditor General, 116, 149
autonomous institutions, 116, 122-124, 130
Avanti, factory, 129
Aztecs, 12

Badajoz, 23
bananas, ix-x, 77-81, 83, 102, 119-120, 124, 129, 133, 138, 157, 161; *see also*: United Fruit Company
Banco Anglo Costarricense, 175-176
banks, 83, 86, 120-121, 124, 168, 173, 175-176; nationalization, 115, 125-126;

privatization, 148-149, 163; reform of 1936, 100; *see also*: credit
Beatles, The 139
Bentham, Jeremy, 61
Bering Straits, 1
Bernard, Eulalia, 137
Bertheau, Margarita, 136
Biehl, John, 149
biodiversity, 159
Bonaparte, Napoleon, 52
Bonilla, Juan José, 47
Boruca, 31
Braun, Werhner von, 158
Brazil, 37
Brazilwood, 48-49
Brenes Mesén, Roberto, 88, 123
Bridge, Walter, 49
Bush, George, 182

cacao, 6, 32-34, 36, 38, 41, 46, 82-83, 120; peso of, 33
cacicazgos, 5-6, 8-10, 12-13, 22; Boruca, 13; Coto, 13; Nicoya, 13, 17; Pococí, 13; Quepo, 13; Suerre, 13; Talamanca, 13; Tariaca, 13; Votos, 13; *see also*: indigenous societies
caciques, 5, 14, 16, 24-26, 35
Caja Costarricense de Seguro Social, *see*: Costa Rican Social Security
Calderocomunismo, 107
Calderón Fournier, Rafael Ángel, 127, 154-155, 161, 165, 179
Calderón Guardia, Rafael Ángel, 102, 104-108, 110-112, 114, 125-128, 154, 156; alliance with Communists, 107; conflict with Cortesistas, 107
Calderón, Antonio, 37
call centers, 164
Calzada, Juan Rafael, 107
camino real, 30
Campaña Nacional (1856-57), *see*: National Campaign
Canada, 159
capitalism, 70, 148, 182; agrarian, 49, 51, 54, 69, 120, 128-129, 151-152; capital accumulation, 49, 124, 143
Caracas, 33
Carazo Odio, Rodrigo, 144, 146, 149, 167
Carballo, Luis, 105
Cardona, Édgar, 125
Carías, Tiburcio, 118
Cariay, 23
Caribbean Basin Initiative, 148
Caribbean Legion, 112-113

Caribbean, 3, 6, 15, 23-24, 30, 35, 41, 56, 77, 83, 102; basin, 33, 36, 78; coast, 23, 46, 79-80, 161, 172; dictatorships, 113-114; islands, 37; jungles, 27; lowlands, 13, 78
Carrillo, Braulio, 55, 57-58
Carrillo, Celia, 88
Cartago, 13, 25-26, 28, 30, 35-41, 45, 52-54, 63, 70, 74-75, 131; council of, 28, 53; Juan Viñas, 81; Tres Ríos, 63; Turrialba, 1-2, 134, 161
Casa de Enseñanza de Santo Tomás, 61
Casa de Moneda (the mint), 48
Castillo de Austria, 24
Castillo de Garcimuñoz, 24
Castro, José María, 66
Catholic Church, 21, 34, 38, 41, 55-56, 58, 70, 75, 89, 104-105, 107-108, 138, 154-155, 170-171, 174; Christ, 104; decline of Catholicism, 170-171; Episcopal Conference of Medellín, 138; God, 26; Holy Week, 48, 170; Jesus, 155; option for the poor, 138; San José, 57; scandals, 171; Second Vatican Council, 138; social Catholicism, 103-105; *see also*: Virgin of los Ángeles
cattle, 29, 31-32, 37-38, 40-41, 45-47, 82-83, 120, 129, 133, 161; beef, 120-121; dairy farming, 120; *see also*: mules
Cavallón, Juan de, 24, 26
census of 2000, 173
Center for the Study of National Problems, 111-112, 116-117, 123
Central America, 6, 11, 19-20, 22, 44, 48, 52, 57, 66, 83, 92, 103, 118, 152-153, 158, 161, 163, 176, 178; Caribbean of, 22; Common Market, 121, 140-141; Conquest, 19-22; crisis of 1930s, 118; crisis of 1980s, 144, 146-148, 150-152; dictatorships, 118, 181; Federal Congress, 53; Federal Republic, 53-54, 56-57; Free Trade Agreement (CAFTA), 178-180; *maras*, 173; militaries, 118; Pacific of, 22, 31, 49; peace plan, 152; social exploitation, 153
Central Bank, 151
Central Valley, 3, 6, 12-13, 15, 24-27, 31, 36, 38-39, 42-45, 47-49, 51, 55, 64-65, 77, 80, 82-84, 101, 108-109, 133, 137, 151, 161
Certificates of Tax Deferral (CATs), 175, 177; *see also*: corruption, organized crime, taxes

Céspedes, Amando, 92
chácara, 40, 43
Chang Díaz, Franklin, 158
Chase, Alfonso, 140
Chibchas, 7
Chic Theater, 168
Chile, 49; Easter Island, 8; elite police (the carabineros), 156; Horn, the, 49
Chome, 34
Ciamba, 23
Ciruro, 34
Civil Service, 116
Civil War of 1948, ix-x, 111, 113-114, 117, 125, 132
class cultures, 172-173
classical music, 95-96, 140, 167
coffee, ix-x, 39, 49-52, 55, 59, 63-66, 68, 77, 80, 82-84, 88, 99, 102, 120, 124, 134, 141, 145, 157-158, 160; beneficios (processing facilities), 50-51, 133; crisis of 1847-49, 66; El Laberinto, 50; elite, 50-51, 65, 68, 83, 106, 111, 115, 127, 164; farmers, 51, 84, 132, 125; farmers against processors, 84, 100, 132; Institute for Defense of Coffee, 100; pickers, 51-52, 63, 99, 134
Cold War, 108, 118, 128, 138
Colombia, 6-7, 56, 78; Cartagena, 30, 33; drug cartels, 177
Columbus, Christopher, 23
Comcel-Millicom, 166
commerce, 22, 27, 29-34, 36, 38, 41-44, 48-50, 65, 77-78, 80, 99, 102, 142, 146, 152, 163, 169, 178-180; see also: contraband, exports
communal lands, 40, 51, 65, 84
Communists, 87-88, 100, 102-108, 110-111, 114, 117, 126, 128-131, 164; see also: left
community organizations, 130-131; mobilizations, 130-131, 149-151
Congress, 58, 76, 87, 93-94, 105, 111, 116; see also: Legislative Assembly
Conquest, x, 8, 11, 13, 18-19, 22-27
Constitution of 1844, 58; of 1848, 59, 74; of 1859, 74; of 1871, 74, 103, 116; of 1949, 115-116, 166
Constitutional Court, 166, 178; civil rights reinforcement, 165-167
contraband, 33, 35, 175
Contraloría General de la República, see: Auditor General
Contreras, Rodrigo de, 23
co-operatives, 125, 128, 133

Cordero, Manuela, 58
Córdova, Santiago, 74
corruption, 77-78, 88, 112, 116, 171, 174-177, 179-180; impact on political system, 177-178; see also: organized crime
Cortés, León, 100, 105, 107, 110, 112
Costa Rica: Province of, 21; State of 54-55
Costa Rica: The Switzerland of Central America, 116
Costa Rican Coalition for Development Initiatives (CINDE), 149
Costa Rican Development Corporation (CODESA), 143, 148
Costa Rican Electricity Institute (ICE), 115, 157, 166, 179; "combo" of, 157, 166
Costa Rican Feminist League, 93-94
Costa Rican Social Security (CCSS), 102-103, 119, 133, 163, 172, 179, 182; see also: health
Costa Rican Tobacco Company, 122
Costa Rican Tourism Institute, 161
Coultas, F. G., 113
credit, 45, 49-50, 68, 83, 115, 120, 125, 143; see also: banks
crisis of 1930s, x, 99-100, 118; of 1980s, 145-149
CR-USA, 153
Cuba, 78; blockade of, 128; revolution, 121
Cubillo, Alonso de, 30
Curaçao, 33

dance, 95, 136, 140; dances, 59, 92, 137
Darío, Rubén, 95, 134
Dean, James, 135
Debravo, Jorge, 133, 137
debt: foreign, 100, 142-143, 147; English, 78; federal, 53; internal, 157, 176
Defensoría de los Habitantes, 166
deficit, 100, 142, 149, 154-155; see also: taxes
Del Monte, 158
democracy, x, 75-76, 85, 94, 103, 116, 118, 125, 127, 147-148, 151, 153, 165-166, 181-182; origin myth, 75-76; rural and classless myth, 39, 151; see also: elections, political parties
Díaz, Hugo, 142
dictatorship of Carrillo, 55-57; of Guardia, 69, 74, 77; of Tinoco, 86, 93
Dirección Nacional de Desarrollo de la Comunidad, see: National Directorate of Community Development
division between city and countryside, 59-62; see also: urban culture

division of labor, 1, 5
Dobles, Fabián, 137
domestic service, 163
domestication of plants, ix, 2-4
Dominican Republic, 178
Drop of Milk, 90, 93
drugs, 97, 139, 174, 176-177; cocaine, 177, heroin, 97; marijuana, 97, 174; morphine, 97; opium, 97
Dunlop, Robert Glasgow, 51

Echandi, Enrique, 67
Echandi, Mario, 124, 126-127
Economically Active Population, 65, 152, 162-163
Ecuador, 6; Guayaquil, 33
Edelman, Marc, 182
education, 19, 60-61, 69-73, 87-88, 90, 93, 95, 107, 123, 137-138, 140, 146, 151, 154, 167-168; privatization, 167, 169, 172; reform of the 1880s, 69-70; secondary, 95, 123, 125, 158; university, 61, 102, 123-125, 139-140, 154-155, 167-168; *see also*: literacy
El Salvador, 11, 47, 53, 57, 63, 118, 144, 146, 173
elections, 73-76, 85, 87, 103-108, 110-113, 116-117, 126-128, 134, 143, 147, 166, 178, 180; census of 1885, 74; federal, 53; franchise, 58-59, 74, 92-94; fraud, 75, 85, 108-109, 111, 113, 116; reforms, 58-59, 74, 85, 93-94, 110, 116, 149, 178; of 1889, 75-76; of 1948, 110-113, 117; turnout, 177-178, 180; *see also*: democracy, political parties
Electoral Registry, 111
encomienda, 22, 26, 34-35, 38
Enlightenment, 61
environment: agro-chemicals, 120, 128-129; costs, 128-129, 134, 160-161, 172; deforestation, 129, 160-161
Espinach, Buenaventura, 51
Esttagny, A., 69
ethnicity, 37, 73-74, 80, 83, 90, 109, 137, 166; blacks, 34, 36-38, 45-46, 80; mestizos, 19, 38, 45, 47; mulattos, 37, 45, 67, 73-74, 109, 137; *pardos*, 45; whites, 38, 45, 72-74, 88, 109, 137, 174; *zambos*, 45; *zambos mosquitos*, 33, 56; *see also*: Afro-Caribbeans, immigration, indigenous societies, slavery
eugenics, 90
Europe, 47, 140, 159; cultural influence, 59-62, 77, 95-97, 134; Iberian Penin-sula, 52; industrial revolution, 47; Pyrenees, 43
exports, 29, 31-33, 38, 41-42, 49-50, 77-78, 80-82, 98-99, 102, 115, 119-120, 125, 128, 141-142, 147, 157, 160, 181; diversification, 81-82, 120-121, 157-158; non traditional, 148, 157-161, 163, 175

Facio Brenes, Rodrigo, 111, 116-117, 123, 180
Factoría de Tabacos, 45
Fallas Sibaja, Carlos Luis, 100, 102, 138
family, 38, 40-41, 43, 45, 50-51, 58, 60, 65, 70-71, 83-84, 92, 100, 106, 131-132, 134, 138, 155, 175, 180; changes of, 171; children, 37, 51, 60, 70-71, 73, 90, 93, 114, 127, 130-131, 133, 161, 164, 171, 182; divorce: 70, 171; domestic violence, 58, 172; young people, 51, 63-64, 88-89, 97, 107, 111, 116-117, 139, 173; *see also*: women
farmers, 39-40, 45, 55, 65, 74, 109, 149, 151, 163; poor, 128, 151-152; small and middling producers or owners, 38, 40, 52, 72, 125, 151-152, 182; *see also*: coffee, peasants
fascism, 108
Faust, 60
Fernández de Córdoba, Francisco, 22
Fernández de Oviedo, Gonzalo, 17
Fernández, Leda, 180
Fernández, Próspero, 69, 74, 78
Figueres Ferrer, José, 111-115, 117-118, 123-124, 126, 128, 140, 155-156, 165
Figueres Olsen, José María, 155, 165, 179; pact with Calderón Fournier, 155-157
films: documentary, 140; feature, 92, 167, 173; *Asesinato en El Meneo*, 167; *Caribe*, 167; *El Retorno*, 92; *Eulalia*, 167; *La Segua*, 167; *Los Secretos de Isolina*, 167; *Marasmo*, 167; *Mujeres Apasionadas*, 167; *Password*, 167, 173
Fischel corporation, 179
foreign capital, 82-83, 120-121, 141-142, 153-154; *see also*: United Fruit Company, INTEL
Formoso, Manuel, 165

Garabito, 26
García Monge, Joaquín, 88
gender inequity, 93, 172; *see also*: women
Germany, 106, 108; Westphalia, 59

globalization, 99, 119, 169, 182; advertisement, 135, 169; American way of life, 169; cable television, 169; cultural impact, 169; Internet, 169; malls, x, 161-162, 169; *see also*: mass culture; media influence

gold, 7, 14, 16-18, 23, 48, 82-83; *see also*: mining, silver

González Dávila, Gil, 22

González Flores, Alfredo, 86

González Víquez, Cleto, 86, 97-98

González, Luisa, 137

González, Manuel de la Cruz, 137

Gounod, Charles, 60

Granda y Balbín, Lorenzo Antonio de, 35

Gross Domestic Product (GDP), 145, 149, 154-155, 157, 159-160, 174-176

Guanacaste, 30-32, 38, 41, 46-47, 55, 74, 80, 82-84, 108, 129, 133-134, 137, 161, 182; Abangares, 83-84, port, 30; Alvarado, port, 30; Bagaces, 31; *cordillera* of, 82; El Viejo, 82; Guardia, 84; Liberia, 71; Nandayure, 30; Nicoya, 6, 13, 17, 20-21, 23, 30-31, 49, 55, 64; Quebrada Grande, 84; Santa Rosa, 67; Tilarán, 84

Guardia Gutiérrez, Tomás, 69, 74, 77

Guatemala, 35, 42-44, 47, 53, 56, 63, 113, 118, 144, 146, 173; Audiencia of Santiago de, 20-21; Kingdom of, 21, 28

Guier, Fernando E., 157

Gulf of Honduras, 11, 20

Gulf of Nicoya, 22

Gutiérrez, Diego, 23-24

Gutiérrez, Felipe, 23

Gutiérrez, Joaquín, 137

Haya Fernández, Diego de la, 31

health, 87, 90, 119, 123, 140, 151, 154; hygiene, 70, 90-91, 93; privatization, 168, 172; *see also*: Costa Rican Social Security

Heredia, 38-40, 45, 52-54, 63, 74-75; Barva, 31; Santo Domingo, 75

Hernández Martínez, Maximiliano, 118

Hernández, Paco, 94

Honduras, 31, 118, 173; Choluteca, 31; Trujillo, 67

Iglesias, Rafael, 76, 85

immigration, 79-80; Chinese, 79, 83; European, 48, 51, 61; illegal, 146, 163; internal, 51-52, 134, 137-138; Italian, 79, 84; Jamaican, 80, 83; law of 2005;

Nicaraguan, 80, 163; 163; *see also*: Afro-Caribbeans

independence, 48, 52-53

Indigenous Dwelling in Sipurio, Talamanca, 15

indigenous societies, ix-x, 1-18; architecture, 9, 11-12, 15-16; astronomy, 8, 12; Bribri, 80; cannibalism, 16-17; chicha, 17; children, 17; commerce, 6, 12, 14, 17; crafts, 4, 7, 9, 12; dances, 17; demographic catastrophe, 19-20, 23; dispossession of the land, 65, 80, 84; epidemic diseases, 19-20, 36; exploitation, 10, 14, 20, 26-27, 31, 34-35, 38; fishing, 1, 4-5, 9; gathering, 1-2, 4-5, 9; genocide of, 20; Huetar, 16; human sacrifice, 16-17; hunting, ix-x, 1-5, 9; kinship, 1, 5, 10, 14-15; languages, 15-16; militaries, 9, 13, 17-18; nobility, 9, 14, 16-17, 22; population, 4-5, 11-12, 18-19, 36, 38, 45; religion, 8, 16; resistance to Conquest, 19-20, 22-27, 38; slavery, 9, 14, 16-17, 20, 22; stone spheres, 8; unequal exchange, 17; uprising of 1709, 35-36; villages, 5, 12, 18; war, 12, 14, 17-18; women, 16-18, 20, 34; workers, 9; *see also*: *cacicazgos, señoríos*

indigo, 29, 47

industry, 83, 88, 101, 120, 125, 129, 146, 161, 163; high-tech companies, 158-160, 168; import-substitution, 101, 121-122, 141-143; *maquila*, 158, 163-164, 172

inflation, 106, 145

institutional change, 114-116, 133, 136, 148-149, 155, 162; *see also*: social reform

Instituto Costarricense de Electricidad, *see*: Costa Rican Electricity Institute

Instituto Costarricense de Turismo, *see*: Costa Rican Tourism Institute

Instituto Nacional de Seguros, *see*: National Insurance Institute

Instituto Tecnológico de Costa Rica, 140

Instrumentarium, 179

INTEL, 158-160

intellectuals, 69, 72, 80, 87-92, 96, 111, 117, 140, 168, 172; loss of radicalism, 164-165; radicalization, 87-89, 92, 96, 139-140

internal market, 44, 48, 65, 82, 120, 125, 151

International Monetary Fund (IMF), 146-148, 157

international relations, 55-56, 66-67, 125-126, 128, 147-148, 150-152
invasion from Nicaragua in 1949, 125; in 1955, 126
Istarú, Ana, 171
Italy, 153

Jamaica, 23, 33, 80
Japan, 108
Jiménez Oreamuno, Ricardo, 85, 97-98, 103
Johnson, Hallett, 108
juntas progresistas, 130

Keith, Minor C., 78, 82
Kissling, Walter, 143

La Loca de Gandoca, 172
Labor Code, 103
land reforms, 84
Latin America, x, 55, 69, 90, 138, 146, 181; dictatorships, 128; guerrilla struggles, 138; *neoliberalismo*, 146
left, the, 104, 129, 132, 140; crisis of, 165; ultra, 151; Western, 153; *see also*: Communists
Legislative Assembly, 139, 149, 166, 172, 178-180; Second Report of the Commission on Drug Trafficking, 176; *see also*: Congress
Liberalism, 61; ideology of progress, 61, 70, 87
Liberals, 67, 69-72, 87, 89-91, 93, 99, 104, 116, 137-138; reforms by, 69-72
Librería Española, 95
Liga Feminista Costarricense, *see*: Costa Rican Feminist League
Limbury, 59
Limón, 23, 78, 80-81, 108, 113, 134, 137; Cahuita, 80; "El Bosque", 100; Gandoca, 161; Matina, 30, 33, 36, 38, 45, 56; Moín, 30; Sixaola, 80; Talamanca, 27, 35-36, 45-46, 65, 80
literacy, 59, 70, 92, 109, 119; *see also*: education
literature, 101-102, 137-138, 171-172
Lizano, Eduardo, 151
Lobo, Tatiana, 171
Long Live Independence, 142
Lubín Barahona and His Caballeros of Rhythm, 92, 135
Luna, Seferino, 37
Lyra, Carmen (María Isabel Carvajal), 88

Mamita Yunai, 102, 138
Maracaibo, 33
Marbella, 23
marches: against CAFTA, 179; against the closing of the Banco Anglo Costarricense, 176; against the "combo ICE", 157; against the reform of the Pension Law, 156; demanding funding for public universities, 154; for CAFTA, 178; for electoral guarantees; 109; for peace, 150-151; in solidarity with banana workers, 140; of unemployed, 100
María Estuardo, 136
Marseillaise, 60
Martén, Alberto, 164-165
Masonry, 61
mass culture, 91-92; comics, 134; football (soccer), 91, 135, 153; local, 92, 135; movies, 91, 134, 169; popular music, 91-92, 135; radio, 91, 134-135, 174; television, 135, 173; *see also*: globalization, media influence
maternalism, 93, 131; Mother's Day, 93
Maternity, 93
Mayas, 7, 11-12
media influence, 103, 109, 135, 138, 179; *see also*: globalization, mass culture, newspapers
Medina, Parmenio, 174
Meinecke, Gustavo, 59
Meléndez, José, 132
merchants, 28, 41-43, 48-50, 52, 109
Mexico, 3, 20-21, 48, 53, 108, 112; Chiapas, 21; Empire, 52-53
middle classes, 97-98, 106, 125, 131, 138, 163, 172; *see also*: farmers, intellectuals
military, 35, 38, 41, 54-55, 57, 67-69, 75, 86-87, 92, 112-113, 150; abolition of the army, 114-115, 126
mining, 23, 48, 82-84, 139
Ministry of Agriculture, 120
Ministry of Culture, Youth and Sports, 136
Ministry of Labor, 90
Ministry of Natural Resources, Energy and Mines (MIRENEM), 161
Ministry of Public Health, 90
Monge Alfaro, Carlos, 111-112
Monge, Luis Alberto, 125, 147, 149-151
Montealegre, Mariano, 45
Montero, Vicente, 58
Montes del Aguacate, 48, 82
Mora Fernández, Juan, 55

Mora, Juan Rafael, 65-68, 74
Mora, Manuel, 87, 106, 108
Mora, Ricardo, 92
Morales, Juan Rafael, 92, 129
Morazán, Francisco, 56-58
Morel de Santa Cruz, Pedro Agustín, 38
Moya, Rigoberto, 96
mules, 30-31, 52, 63; *see also*: cattle
municipal government, 28, 55, 60, 76, 87, 172; *cabildos*, 52-53; fragmented sovereignty, 52
Munro, Dana Gardner, x, 87
My Hygiene Catechism, 90

national anthem, 60, 88
National Archive, 95
National Campaign, 66-68, 72, 180; cholera, 68
National Child Welfare Bureau, 90
National Directorate of Community Development (DINADECO), 130
National Electoral Tribunal, 113
national identity 72-73, 86-87, 92, 101, 137; crisis of, 174
National Insurance Institute, 179
National Library, 95
National Museum, 8, 95
National Theater, 60-61, 95
neoliberalismo, 146, 165, 180, 182
neoliberals, x, 149, 151, 153-154, 162, 166, 175, 178, 180; ascendancy within PLN, 149; "shock therapy" 154-155
neutrality, 151
New Spain, Viceroyalty of, 21
newspapers, 60, 88, 91, 95; *Álbum Semanal*, 59; *Diario de Costa Rica*, 110; *El Ferrocarril*, 78; *La Nación*, 131, 153, 163, 167; *La Prensa Libre*, 75; *Nuestra Voz*; 131; *Trabajo*, 103; *see also*: media influence; print culture
Nicaragua, x, 13, 20, 24, 29-32, 42, 44, 49, 55-56, 66, 79-80, 118, 125-126, 144, 146, 150, 169, 177; Contra guerrillas, 177; El Realejo, 29; Granada, 24, 29; Lake Nicaragua, 66; Leon, 29, 43, 56; Rivas, 67-68; Sandinistas, 144, 146-147, 150-153; San Juan River, 14, 66-67; Somoza dictatorship, 118, 146
Nicoya: annexation of Partido de, 55; Corregimiento of, 21; *see also*: Guanacaste
Nicuesa, Diego de, 23
Numar, 121

number of people per vehicle, 162
Núñez, Solón, 90

Ochomogo, battle of, 53-54
Odio, Rubén, 123
Oduber Quirós, Daniel, 124, 128, 140, 143, 158
on-line gambling, 164
Organization of American States (OAS), 125-126
organized crime, 173-174; auto theft, 173; money laundering, 176-177; *see also*: corruption, drugs, prostitution
Orlich Bolmarcich, Francisco, 131
ornamental plants, 158

Pacaca, 34
Pacheco de la Espriella, Abel, 178-180
Pacheco, Fausto, 101
Pacific Railway, 83
Pacific, 47, 64, 77; coast, 22, 30, 65, 78; north, 3-4, 12-15, 17, 22, 24, 30, 37; south, 6, 8, 13, 15, 35, 81, 102, 133, 145
Pacto del Caribe, 113-114
Palacios, Matías, 34
Panama, 6-7, 20-21, 30-31, 42-43, 55, 66, 79, 86; Audiencia of, 28; Bocas del Toro, 21, 24, 55; Canal, 78; Nombre de Dios, 30; Portobelo, 30, 33
parks and natural reserves, 159
Patronato Nacional de la Infancia, *see*: National Child Welfare Bureu
Pavlova, Ana, 95
peasants, 37-40, 42, 45-48, 51-52, 62-64, 67, 70, 75, 81, 83, 86, 91, 102, 116, 174; disappearance of, 151-152; discontent of, x, 51, 65, 84, 132-133, 151-152; exploitation of, 42-43; poor, 40-41, 48, 51, 65, 83-84, 109, 128, 132-133; *see also*: farmers
pension reform, 156-157
Peru, 20, 28, 30
Picado, Teodoro, 108, 110
pirates, 33
Piza Escalante, Rodolfo, 166
plastic arts, 101, 137, 140, 167
political instability, 53-55, 68-69, 107-114, 125-127; coup d'etat of 1859, 68, 74; of 1917, 86
political parties, 73-74, 76, 85, 87, 94, 113, 166, 172, 180; Citizens' Action Party (PAC), 180; Democratic Action Party, 112; Libertarian Movement,

180; National Republican Party, 103, 105, 107; Party of National Liberation (PLN), 117-118, 120, 124, 126-128, 136, 140, 143, 147, 149, 151, 155, 177-180; Reformist Party, 87; Social Christian Unity Party (PUSC), 149, 154-155, 157, 177-178, 180; Social Democratic Party, 112; two-party system, 149, 180; Unity Coalition, 149; Vanguardia Popular Party, 108, 111; *see also*: democracy, elections, Communists

Ponce de León, Hernán, 22

popular culture, 69-71, 89-92, 96; cockfight, 59-60, 71; *see also*: mass culture

popular uprising of 1842, 57; of 7 November 1889, 75

population, 39, 45-47, 52, 72, 80, 90, 109, 116, 137, 155, 164, 166-167, 170-171, 174, 182; demographic transition, 171

Povedano, Tomás, 66

poverty, 27, 38, 60, 65, 88, 90, 96, 108, 134, 138, 145, 154-155, 170, 173-176; *see also*: farmers, peasants

Presbere, Pablo, 35-36

presidential re-election, 178

Presley, Elvis, 135

print culture, 60-61, 91; books, 59-61, 91, 95; *see also*: newspapers

printing press, 60

privatization of land, 49-51, 55, 58, 65, 71, 82-84

proclamation of the republic, 54, 59

prostitution, 96, 173

Protestantism, 80, 169-170

Puerto Rico, 78

Puntarenas, 49, 65, 74, 83, 108, 113, 134, 137; Caldera, 30-31, 57; Esparza, 14, 28, 30-32; Juan Solano, shipyard, 30; La Barranca, shipyard, 30; Landecho, 24; Los Reyes, 24; Quepos, 31

Quepo, 34

racial mixture, 33, 37-38

racism, 80, 90, 137-138; *see also*: eugenics, immigration

railroads, 64, 77-79, 83, 154, 161

Rávago, Juan de Estrada, 24

Reagan, Ronald, 147, 150, 182

remittances of Costa Ricans resident abroad, 158-159

Repertorio Americano, 88

repression of 1962 in Cartago, 131

Reventazón, valley of the, 64, 83

Rivera, Perafán de, 26, 34

Rockefeller Foundation, 90

Rodríguez Echeverría, Miguel Ángel, 157, 179-180

Rodríguez, Eugenio, 179

Rodríguez, José Joaquín, 75-76, 85

Rossi, Ana Cristina, 161, 172

Rossi, Jorge, 120

Russia, 104, 108; *see also*: Soviet Union

Sala Constitucional (Sala Cuarta), *see*: Constitutional Court

Sala Garbo, 169

Salazar, Margarita, 133

Salazar, Melico, 96

salt, 6, 9, 29, 34

San José, x, 14, 37-40, 45, 48-49, 52-54, 56-66, 74-75, 94-95, 97, 99-100, 107-108, 111, 113-114, 116, 123, 126, 133-135, 139-141, 145, 150-153, 155, 162, 167, 174; Alto de Guadalupe, 169; Aserrí, 31; Candelaria, 40; Cathedral, 56; Central Park, 57; Desamparados, 174-175; San Ignacio de Acosta, 110; San Isidro de El General, 113; Second Company, 140; Tarrazú, 64; Tibás, 123

San Pedro Mall, 162

Sanabria, Víctor Manuel, 104-108, 138

Sánchez de Badajoz, Hernán, 23

Sánchez, Juan Manuel, 101, 137

Sancho, Mario, 116

Sanclemente, Luis, 15

Santamaría, Juan, 67-68, 70, 72-73

Saprissa Textile Factory, 141

Sarapiquí, 45

Schiller, Friedrich von, 136

scientists, 88, 96, 140

Scotland, 153

seafood, 158

Second Republic, 115-116, 118; *Junta Fundadora* of the, 114-117, 125

secularization, 58, 61, 69-72, 91, 170-171

Segura, Gerónimo, 68

señoríos, 13; Garabito, 13-14, 16; Guarco, 13-14, 16; *see also*: *cacicazgos*, indigenous societies

Serrat, Joan Manuel, 139

Shakespeare, William, 59

silver, 33, 48, 82; *see also*: gold

slavery, 35-38, 41, 46; resistance to, 36

Smith, Adam, 61

So You Want to Be a Rocket Scientist, 158

social conflicts, x, 65, 83-84, 89, 130-133;

139-140, 145, 149-152, 154, 156-157, 176, 179-180; dealing conflict with legal forms, 40, 58, 84-85, 133, 151; *see also*: peasants, strikes, workers
Social Guarantees, 103
social inequity, 39, 97-98, 173-174, 181; Gini coefficient, 173
social justice, 92, 118, 125, 164, 174, 181-182
social policies, 87, 89-90, 93, 119, 123, 151, 154, 182
social question, 88, 104; *see also*: poverty
social reform, 102-107, 110-111, 114-115
socialism, 61, 88, 91, 112
Society of Artisans of Costa Rica, 85
Solano Astaburuaga, Francisco, 52
Solano, Dominga, 37
solidarismo, 164-165
Solís, Javier, 138
Solís, Juan Vicente, 107
Solís, Ottón, 180
Somoza Debayle, Anastasio, 146
Somoza García, Anastasio, 118
Soto, Bernardo, 69, 75
South America, 2-3
Soviet Union, 107-108, 126, 153; Moscow, 164; *see also*: Russia
Spain, 28; Bourbon reforms, 43-44; Catalonia, 51; Civil War, 104; Constitution of Cadiz, 52, 58; Crown, 26, 33-34, 44
Spanish America, 52
Spanish-American War, 78
Spencer, Joseph, 80
squatters, 128, 132-133
state, 69, 84-85, 118, 120, 122, 129-130, 138, 143, 149, 151, 155, 163, 165-166, 170, 172, 175-176, 180, 182; centralization of political power, 55-58; employees, 100, 114, 122-125, 146, 154-155, 162; entrepreneur, 143; expansion, 69, 89-90, 122-123, 125, 130-131, 133, 136, 140, 162, 166, 168, 175; intervention, 83-84, 87, 89-91, 99-100, 102-103, 120, 123-124, 134; "parallel", 148-149; privatization of, 146, 148, 155-157, 167-168, 176, 178, 180; official culture institutionalization, 136-137; welfare, 103, 155, 175, 180
Stephens, John Lloyd, 47, 63
Stonehenge, 7
strikes, 83-84, 89, 132, 149, 154; *de Brazos Caídos*, 110; of 1920, 89; of 1934, 100
student movement, 132, 138-140; protest of the 24th of April 1970, 139

Sue, Eugène, 61
Suerre River, 24; port, 30
sugar, 38, 40, 44, 81-83, 120-121; *trapiche*, 44, 81; *ingenio*, 81-82
Supreme Electoral Tribunal, 116
Sweden, 153

taxes, 33, 43-44, 49, 86, 99, 115, 126, 143, 152, 154-155, 174; direct taxation, 86, 174; evasion, 143, 174-175; exemptions, 142, 154; *see also*: Certificates of Tax Deferral (CATs), deficit
Teatro Mora, 59
technology, 11, 26, 40, 45, 50, 65, 81, 97, 120, 140, 142, 158, 168
The Burning of the Mesón, 67
The Gorillas, 132
The Heart of Humanity, 91
The Paperboy, 96
The Tragedy of Costa Rica, 114
theater, 59-61, 91-92, 95, 136, 140
Third World, 119, 182
Tinoco, Federico, 86, 93
Tinoco, Joaquín, 86, 93
tobacco, 38, 44-45, 121-122
Tomás Guardia Gutiérrez, 69
tourism, ix-x, 159-161, 163, 169, 172-173
Tratado de Libre Comercio (TLC), *see*: Central American Free Trade Agreement
Tribunal Supremo de Elecciones, *see*: Supreme Electoral Tribunal
Tuarco, 16
Turrialba, valley of, 64, 83

Ubico, Jorge, 118
Ulate, Otilio, 110, 112-114, 117, 126, 128
unequal exchange, 41-43
unions, 88, 92, 103, 125, 132-133; crisis of, 164-165; policies against, 129, 165
United Fruit Company, 78-82, 100, 102, 111, 115, 120-121, 132, 145
United States, 63, 66, 78, 91, 95, 102, 106-108, 118, 121, 126, 128, 135, 140, 142, 147-148, 152, 158-159, 169-170, 177-178; Agency for International Development (AID), 148-149, 153; Alaska, 126; Alliance for Progress, 141; Boston, 78; Central American policy, 147-148, 150-152; Central Intelligence Agency (CIA), 177; Committee on Foreign Relations of the United States Congress, 128; Embassy in San José, 107, 111, 150; imperialism, 78-80; Irangate scandal, 177; Miami,

169; National Aeronautics and Space Administration (NASA), 158; New York, 99; stock market crash of 1929, 99; war on drugs, 177; Washington, 78-79, 128, 148, 151-153; White House, 147
universal male suffrage, 74; female, 116
Universidad Estatal a Distancia, 140
Universidad Nacional Autónoma, 140
University of Costa Rica, 102, 117, 119, 123, 136, 177, 179; Annual National Poll, 177; Student Federation, 132; Theater, 136
University of Santo Tomás, 61
urban culture, 59-62, 94-96, 134, 169; expansion, 134, 161, 173; residential segregation, 172-173; world, ix, 40, 83, 88, 109, 130, 133, 174

Vanegas, Nardo, 130
Variedades theater, 92
Vázquez de Coronado, Juan, 12, 16, 25-26
Villa Bruselas, 22
Villa de la Concepción, 23
village community, 40, 58, 62; conflicts, 40
Virgin of los Ángeles, 57, 70, 73, 104
Volio, Jorge, 87

wage labor, 50, 52, 65, 80, 83, 88, 100, 128, 151, 163
Walker, William, 66-68
War of the League, 54
war with Panama, 86, 93
water, 40, 51, 130-131, 150, 173
Weisinger, Nina, 91
women, 51, 57-58, 93-95, 109, 114, 116, 128, 130-131, 137, 169, 171-173; feminist movement, 172; feminization of teaching, 93; franchise, 93-94, 116; workers, 94, 122, 133, 164, 171-172; *see also*: family, gender inequity
Women's Vote – the Day That They Get It, 94
workers, x, 30, 52, 55, 65, 68, 70, 79-80, 83, 85-91, 96, 99-103, 125, 128, 151, 154, 158, 163-166, 169, 174, 178; banana, 84, 87, 100, 109, 129, 132, 140; culture, 88-89, 91, 129; May Day, 88-89; mining, 84; rights deterioration, 163-164, 172; urban, 84-85, 87-88, 91-92, 96-97, 100, 122, 129, 132, 145; *see also*: artisans, social conflicts, unions, women
World Bank, 157
World Cup of 1990, 153

World War I (1914-18), 79
World War II (1939-45), 79, 102, 107-108, 119

Yucatan Peninsula, 11

Zapatería Francesa, 62
Zeledón, Estrella, 144
Zeledón, José María, 88
Zúñiga, Francisco, 93, 101, 137

AUTHORS

Steven Palmer is Canada Research Chair in History of International Health and Associate Professor in the Department of History at the University of Windsor, Canada. He is the author of *From Popular Medicine to Medical Populism: Doctors, Healers, and Public Power in Costa Rica, 1800-1940*.

Iván Molina is a Professor of History at the Escuela de Historia and a Researcher at the Centro de Investigación en Identidad y Cultura Latinoamericanas (CIICLA), both at the University of Costa Rica. Among his books are *La estela de la pluma. Cultura impresa e intelectuales en Centroamérica durante los siglos XIX y XX* y *La miel de los mudos y otros cuentos ticos de ciencia ficción*.

Books by Molina and Palmer have been reviewed by important academic journals, like *Hispanic American Historical Review*, *The American Historical Review*, *Journal of Latin American Studies*, *The Americas, Annales. Histoire, Sciences Sociales*, *Mesoamérica, Colonial Latin American Historical Review, Bulletin of Latin American Research,* and *The New York Review of Books*.

Questions and comments on this book? Write to:

Steven Palmer
Department of History
University of Windsor
401 Sunset
Windsor, ON
Canada N9B 3P4
spalmer@uwindsor.ca

Iván Molina
Escuela de Historia
Universidad de Costa Rica
San José, Costa Rica
Central America
ivanm@cariari.ucr.ac.cr

Palmer and Molina are coauthors of *Educando a Costa Rica. Alfabetización popular, formación docente y género (1880-1950)*; *La voluntad radiante. Cultura impresa, magia y medicina en Costa Rica (1897-1932)*; and *Costa Rica del siglo XX al XXI. Historia de una sociedad.* They have coedited *Héroes al gusto y libros de moda. Sociedad y cambio cultural en Costa Rica (1750-1900)*; *El paso del cometa. Estado, política social y culturas populares en Costa Rica (1800-1950)*; and *The Costa Rica Reader. History, Culture, Politics.*

Printed by SIEDIN in March 2014

IG-421